Breaking Bread

Breaking Bread

Insurgent Black Intellectual Life

by

bell hooks and Cornel West

South End Press   **Boston, MA**

The cover art is of a 19th century Ethiopian guardian angel. The angel is called upon to maintain a constant vigil against Satan and his minions at each person's right side. (From *Ethiopian Magic Scrolls* by Jacques Mercier.)

Cover design by Sheila Walsh, Tanya Mckinnon and G. Watkins
Text design and production by the South End Press collective and Tanya Mckinnon
Manufactured in the U.S.A.
printed on acid-free paper
Library of Congress Catalog Card Number: 91-22027
Library of Congress Cataloging-in-Publication Data
hooks, bell and West, Cornel
Breaking Bread: Insurgent Black Intellectual Life
1. Afro-American intellectuals. 2. Afro-American—intellectuals interviews. 3. Afro-American—intellectual life. I. West, Cornel. II. Title.

E185.86.H735 1991   973'.0496073--dc20   91-22027

ISBN 0-89608-414-0 (paper)
ISBN 0-89608-415-9 (hard)

South End Press, 116 Saint Botolph St., Boston, MA 02115

99 98 97 96 95 94 93 92   3 4 5 6 7 8 9

Dedications

I dedicate this book to all of us who share a vision of transformative redemptive love between Black women and men. Such love was expressed in the work between Cornel and myself; in the disciplined and dedicated labor, the intellectual insight and commitment our editor, Tanya Mckinnon, gave this work.

We hope that our collective commitment to love as an action and a practice will inspire and/or affirm passionate, progressive, intellectual work on Black experience.

—bh

To my beloved

grandmothers

Lovie O'Gwynn and Rose Bias

—CW

Table of Contents

Introduction

To be sensual...is to respect and rejoice in the force of life, of life itself, and to be present in all that one does, from the effort of loving to the breaking of bread.

James Baldwin
The Fire Next Time

bh The exciting aspect of these dialogues and conversations between Cornel and myself is that they have a quality of testimony. I am sitting here with James Cone's book *My Soul Looks Back* and he says, "Testimony is an integral part of the Black religious tradition. It is the occasion where the believer stands before the community of faith in order to give account of the hope that is in him or her. Although testimony is unquestionably personal and thus primarily an individual story it is also a story accessible to others in the community of faith. Indeed the purpose of testimony is not only to strengthen an individual's faith but also to build a faith of the community."

That spirit of testimony is a very hard spirit to convey in written text, so when I began to think about you and me actually doing more dialogues together than the one we did at Yale, which was our first dialogue, it struck me that dialogue was one of the ways where that sense of mutual witness and testimony could be made manifest. I link that sense to regular communion service in the Black church at Yale where we would often stand in a collective circle and sing, "Let Us Break Bread Together on Our Knees," and the lines in the song which say, "When I Fall on My Knees with My

Face to the Rising Sun, Oh Lord Have Mercy on Me." I liked the combination of the notion of community which is about sharing and breaking bread together, of dialogue as well as mercy because mercy speaks to the need we have for compassion, acceptance, understanding, and empathy.

Cornel, you and I have brought to our relationship as friends and comrades in struggle the willingness to love compassionately, the willingness to engage intellectually with the kind of critical affirmation where we can talk, argue, disagree, even become disappointed in each other, yet still leave one another with a sense of spiritual joy and renewal. Hence our desire to share these discussions with other people, with a community of faith, not to necessarily invoke a religious community, but a community of comrades who are seeking to deepen our spiritual experience and our political solidarity, and others of us seeking primarily to deepen our understanding of Black life and Black political experience.

This is why we want to start with this sense of communion and breaking bread, of sharing fundamentally that which is most one's own. Sharing the word.

CW At the same time there is a wonderful song by Fred Wesley and the JBs entitled "Breaking Bread," and it has to do with a critical recovery and a critical revision of one's past, of one's tradition, of one's history, of one's heritage. As we enter the 1990s, it's very clear that Black people must indeed accent the best of our tradition if we are to make it as a people into the 21st century. There are tremendous impediments and obstacles, very difficult circumstances and conditions, but the breaking bread that could lead toward our critical understanding of the past and present and our transformation of the present into a better future seems to be so very important, and therefore this dialogical form of two intellectuals coming together, trying to take quite seriously the love ethic in its dialogical and intellectual form, is crucial. Now, in many ways, people could suggest the dialogue is a certain analog to improvisation. We know jazz as the major art form created by Black folks. This tradition could, in some way, be enacted in the dialogical form much more easily than on the written page. That isn't to say it's impossible to do it on the written page, but dialogue speaks more intimately to people's lived realities.

bh One of my major mentors Paulo Freire, the Brazilian educator, always says that it is dialogue that is the true act of love between two subjects, and points out again and again, drawing on

Che Guevara and others, that there can be no revolution without love.

Another reason we considered having this dialogue was to think in terms of what forms of writing are more accessible to a mass audience. Both Cornel and I are in academic settings, so that much of the work that we do is published in long manuscript form or in the form of critical essays in academic journals that many people never buy or read. So, the hope in doing this kind of book is to simulate our regular conversations in everyday life. One could ostensibly pick up this book, read a part of it one day and read another part of it the next day without having the continuity of thought destroyed because, like everyday conversation, the dialogue has moments that are fragmented, even as it has thoughts which are contained and concise.

I was very moved by the book Freire did with Antonio Faundez, *Learning to Question*. That was the first book of dialogues to theoretically introduce me to the notion of collectivity. And one of the things I've been thinking about as an intellectual, as a Black woman intellectual revolutionary thinker, is what does it mean to engage some kind of collaborative response? What does it mean for us to talk to one another? In the past few years, especially among Black critical thinkers and writers, there's been a great deal of jockeying for positions between Black women and Black men. There has been a kind of proliferation of the false notion that if Black women are being heard, Black men's voices are necessarily silenced, and if Black men's voices are heard, Black women must assume a voiceless position.

Partly, Cornel and I conceived of the initial dialogue we did together in a public setting as a way to intervene on the kind of sexist divisions that have been historically constructed between Black men and Black women. To present ourselves as living examples of the will on the part of both Black men and women to talk with one another, to process, and engage in rigorous intellectual and political dialogue.

CW At a time when there are so many storms raging and winds blowing in Black male and female relations, it is important to at least take a moment and look, see, examine, question, and scrutinize a particular Black male intellectual and a particular Black female intellectual who are grappling together, struggling together, rooted in a very rich Black tradition but also critical of that tradition such that the best of that tradition can remain alive. *Breaking Bread* is essentially this wrestling with the past and present, wrestling with theory and practice, wrestling with politics and spirituality so that our lives can be richer and our society more just.

bh When I think back to the words of the song "When I Fall on my Knees," it evokes for me the necessity for humility, the sense that it is only when we bow down in a religious sense, when we humble ourselves, that we can be more open. There is a way in which these conversations demand a quality of humility that opposes the hubris which often informs sitting in isolation and writing an essay. Not much of this discussion has been significantly altered, it has not been redone to represent us in a contrived way, and yet when both of us are working on long manuscripts there is that consciousness always of how one is being represented. So there is a certain kind of vulnerability that enters into our dialogue here and our sharing of that dialogue with a more expansive public. In our dialogue we talk about the need for vulnerability as one of the conditions for intimacy but, in fact, it is very hard for academics who are often isolated to accept placing themselves in roles where they might be emotionally vulnerable. I think it is important for readers to know that Cornel and I are friends. There is something about the nature of working in friendship that also makes this dialogue possible and that if we were people who were solely in political solidarity without the context of friendship some of the magic and the sillinesses that appear in our discussion might not be there. It is partially friendship that makes certain forms of vulnerability possible, certain forms of interrogation possible. At certain points I really feel like Cornel sensitively interrogates me around areas which I find myself much more reticent to speak publicly about and I, on occasion, push him to reveal and discuss points of contradiction in his life. We engage in a kind of playful interrogation that is part of a *joie de vivre* we want to bring to our sense of what it means to be Black intellectuals at this historical moment.

CW This kind of humble example can empower other persons who take the life of the mind seriously and link it to spiritual and political struggle. Historically, academic intellectuals have been viewed, to varying degrees, as elitist, arrogant, and haughty, yet these days in which the academic "star system" highlights only one or two Black intellectuals at a time, we see emerging a glass menagerie of the academy. It is important to break down that kind of image and reveal oneself, lay bare some of the very, very important faults and foibles as well as some of the insights and contributions that both of us have made in our past and hope to make in the future.

bh As a cultural critic, I often find myself dogging out Black cultural productions and books that I feel don't cover issues that I want to see covered. I frequently complain, saying, "This book really didn't deal with the subject that I wanted it to deal with, or it didn't really say anything new about a particular issue." What's exciting about these dialogues is that we have tried to use Toni Morrison's phrase "Give voice to the 'unspeakable'" because there are so many aspects of Black life that we talk about in private that we don't really find talked about in books or essays anywhere. So many things about ourselves never get said because when you are writing a regular book-length manuscript, you tend to be projecting toward a wide audience. You ask yourself if a wider audience will really be interested in the question of Black self-esteem or the many myriad issues we bring up here, like my love for Otis Redding's music, our mutual love and respect for the music of Marvin Gaye, because, to some extent, they are real intimacies. These dialogues speak to Black people and Black people should be able to recognize our own shared experience in them in ways that are really vital. One question that came up as we tried to center Blackness in these dialogues is the question of the non-Black reader. I think the invitation offered the non-Black reader is to join us in this expression of our familiarity and via that joining, come to understand that when Black people come together to celebrate and rejoice in Black critical thinking, we do so not to exclude or to separate, but to participate more fully in a world community. However, we must first be able to dialogue with one another, to give one another that subject-to-subject recognition that is an act of resistance that is part of the decolonizing, anti-racist process. So to some extent, we invite all readers then to rejoice with us that this subject-to-subject encounter can be possible within a White supremacist, capitalist, patriarchal context that would, in fact, have us not be capable of talking to one another.

CW That our conversation has principally Black points of reference must be accented. We are looking at the predicament of Black people from the vantage point of all that Africa, Asia, the Middle East, Latin America, and Europe have to offer. We are rooted in that Black tradition and we are struggling with that Black predicament. This does not mean that we subscribe to an exclusive Afro-centricity, though we are centered on the African American situation. Nor does it mean that we valorize, that we promote a

Euro-centric perspective, though we recognize that so much of the academy remains under the sway of a very narrow Euro-centrism. Instead we recognize Black humanity and attempt to promote the love, affirmation, and critique of Black humanity, and in that sense, we attempt to escape the prevailing mode of intellectual bondage that has held captive so many Black intellectuals of the past.

bh In evoking that sense of breaking bread, we call upon the various traditions of sharing that take place in domestic, secular, and sacred life where we come together to give of ourselves to one another fully, to nurture life, to renew our spirits, sustain our hope, and to make a lived politics of revolutionary struggle an ongoing practice.

1

Black Women And Men: partnership in the 1990s

a dialogue between bell hooks and Cornel West presented at Yale University's African American Cultural Center

Give gifts to those who should know love.

Ntozake Shange
Sassafrass, Cypress, and Indigo

The history of the period has been written and will continue to be written without us. The imperative is clear: Either we will make history or remain the victims of it.

Michele Wallace

bh I requested that Charles sing "Precious Lord" because the conditions that led Thomas Dorsey to write this song always make me think about gender issues, issues of Black masculinity. Mr. Dorsey wrote this song after his wife died in childbirth. That experience caused him to have a crisis of faith. He did not think he would be able to go on living without her. That sense of unbearable crisis truly expresses the contemporary dilemma of faith. Mr. Dorsey talked about the way he tried to cope with this "crisis of faith." He prayed and prayed for a healing and received the words to this song. This song has helped so many folk when they are feeling low, feeling as if they can't go on. It was my grandmother's favorite song. I remember how we sang it at her funeral. She died when she was almost ninety. And I am moved now as I was then by the knowledge that we can take our pain, work with it, recycle it, and transform it so that it becomes a source of power.

Let me introduce to you my "brother," my comrade Cornel West.

CW First I need to just acknowledge the fact that we as Black people have come together to reflect on our past, present, and future. That, in and of itself, is a sign of hope. I'd like to thank the Yale African American Cultural Center for bringing us together. bell and I thought it would be best to present in dialogical form a series of reflections on the crisis of Black males and females. There is a state of siege raging now in Black communities across this nation linked not only to drug addiction but also to consolidation of corporate power as we know it, and redistribution of wealth from the bottom to the top, coupled with the ways with which a culture and society centered on the market, preoccupied with consumption, erode structures of feeling, community, tradition. Reclaiming our heritage and sense of history are prerequisites to any serious talk about Black freedom and Black liberation in the 21st century. We want to try to create that kind of community here today, a community that we hope will be a place to promote understanding. Critical understanding is a prerequisite for any serious talk about coming together, sharing, participating, creating bonds of solidarity so that Black people and other progressive people can continue to hold up the blood-stained banners that were raised when that song was sung in the civil rights movement. It was one of Dr. Martin Luther King's favorite songs, reaffirming his own struggle and that of many others who have tried to link some sense of faith, religious faith, political faith, to the struggle for freedom. We thought it would be best to have a dialogue to put forth analysis and provide a sense of what form a praxis would take. That praxis will be necessary for us to talk seriously about Black power, Black liberation in the 21st century.

bh Let us say a little bit about ourselves. Both Cornel and I come to you as individuals who believe in God. That belief informs our message.

CW One of the reasons we believe in God is due to the long tradition of religious faith in the Black community. I think, that as a people who have had to deal with the absurdity of being Black in America, for many of us it is a question of God and sanity, or God and suicide. And, if you are serious about Black struggle, you know that in many instances you will be stepping out on nothing, hoping to land on something. That is the history of Black folks in the past and present, and it continually concerns those of us who are willing to speak out with boldness and a sense of the importance of history and struggle. You speak, knowing that you won't be able to do that for too long because America is such a violent culture. Given those conditions, you have to ask yourself what links to a tradition will sustain you, given the absurdity and insanity we are bombarded with daily. And so the belief in God itself is not to be understood in a noncontextual manner. It is understood in relation to a particular context, to specific circumstances.

bh We also come to you as two progressive Black people on the Left.

CW Very much so.

bh I will read a few paragraphs to provide a critical framework for our discussion of Black power, just in case some of you may not know what Black power means. We are gathered to speak with one another about Black power in the 21st century. In James Boggs's essay, "Black Power: A Scientific Concept Whose Time Has Come," first published in 1968, he called attention to the radical political significance of the Black power movement, asserting: "Today the concept of Black power expresses the revolutionary social force which must not only struggle against the capitalist but against the workers and all who benefit by and support the system which has oppressed us." We speak of Black power in this very different context to remember, reclaim, re-vision, and renew. We remember first that the historical struggle for Black liberation was forged by Black women and men who were concerned about the collective welfare of Black people. Renewing our commitment to this collective struggle should provide a grounding for new direction in contemporary political practice. We speak today of political partnership between Black men and women. The late James Baldwin wrote in his autobiographical preface to *Notes of a Native Son:* "I think that the past is all that makes the present coherent and further that the past will remain horrible for as long as we refuse to accept it honestly." Accepting the challenge of this prophetic statement as we look at our contemporary past as Black people, the space between the sixties and the nineties, we see a weakening of political solidarity between Black men and women. It is crucial for the future of Black liberation struggle that we remain ever mindful that ours is a shared struggle, that we are each other's fate.

CW I think we can even begin by talking about the kind of existentialist chaos that exists in our own lives and our inability to overcome the sense of alienation and frustration we experience when we try to create bonds of intimacy and solidarity with one another. Now part of this frustration is to be understood again in relation to structures and institutions. In the way in which our culture of consumption has promoted an addiction to stimulation—one that puts a premium on packaged and commodified stimulation. The market does this in order to convince us that our consumption keeps oiling the economy in order for it to reproduce itself. But the effect of this addiction to stimulation is an undermining, a waning of our ability for qualitatively rich relationships. It's no accident that crack is the postmodern drug, that it is the highest form of addiction known to humankind, that it provides a feeling ten times more pleasurable than orgasm.

bh Addiction is not about relatedness, about relationships. So it comes as no surprise that, as addiction becomes more pervasive in Black life, it undermines our capacity to experience community. Just recently, I was telling someone that I would like to buy a little house next door to my parent's house. This house used to be Mr. Johnson's house but he recently passed away. And they could not understand why I would want to live near my parents. My explanation that my parents were aging did not satisfy. Their inability to understand or appreciate the value of sharing family life intergenerationally was a sign to me of the crisis facing our communities. It's as though as Black people we have lost our understanding of the importance of mutual interdependency, of communal living. That we no longer recognize as valuable the notion that we collectively shape the terms of our survival is a sign of crisis.

CW And when there is crisis in those communities and institutions that have played a fundamental role in transmitting to younger generations our values and sensibility, our ways of life and our ways of struggle, we find ourselves distanced, not simply from our predecessors but from the critical project of Black liberation. And so, more and more, we seem to have young Black people who are very difficult to understand, because it seems as though they live in two very different worlds. We don't really understand their music. Black adults may not be listening to NWA (Niggers With Attitude) straight out of Compton, California. They may not understand why they are doing what Stetsasonic is doing, what Public Enemy is all about, because most young Black people have been fundamentally shaped by the brutal side of American society. Their sense of reality is shaped on the one hand by a sense of coldness and callousness, and on the other hand by a sense of

passion for justice, contradictory impulses which surface simultaneously. Mothers may find it difficult to understand their children.
Grandparents may find it difficult to understand us—and it's this
slow breakage that has to be restored.

bh That sense of breakage, or rupture, is often tragically expressed in gender relations. When I told folks that Cornel West and
I were talking about partnership between Black women and men,
they thought I meant romantic relationships. I replied that it was
important for us to examine the multi-relationships between Black
women and men, how we deal with fathers, with brothers, with
sons. We are talking about all our relationships across gender because it is not just the heterosexual love relationships between
Black women and men that are in trouble. Many of us can't communicate with parents, siblings, etc. I've talked with many of you
and asked, "What is it you feel should be addressed?" And many of
you responded that you wanted us to talk about Black men and
how they need to "get it together."

Let's talk about why we see the struggle to assert agency—
that is, the ability to act in one's best interest—as a male thing. I
mean, Black men are not the only ones among us who need to "get
it together." And if Black men collectively refuse to educate themselves for critical consciousness, to acquire the means to be self-de-
termined, should our communities suffer, or should we not
recognize that both Black women and men must struggle for self-
actualization, must learn to "get it together"? Since the culture we
live in continues to equate Blackness with maleness, Black awareness of the extent to which our survival depends on mutual partnership between Black women and men is undermined. In
renewed Black liberation struggle, we recognize the position of
Black men and women, the tremendous role Black women played
in every freedom struggle.

Certainly, Septima Clark's book *Ready from Within* is necessary reading for those of us who want to understand the historical
development of sexual politics in Black liberation struggle. Clark
describes her father's insistence that she not fully engage herself in
civil rights struggle because of her gender. Later, she found the
source of her defiance in religion. It was the belief in spiritual community, that no difference must be made between the role of
women and that of men, that enabled her to be "ready within." To
Septima Clark, the call to participate in Black liberation struggle
was a call from God. Remembering and recovering the stories of
how Black women learned to assert historical agency in the strug-

gle for self-determination in the context of community and collectivity is important for those of us who struggle to promote Black
liberation, a movement that has at its core a commitment to free
our communities of sexist domination, exploitation, and oppression. We need to develop a political terminology that will enable
Black folks to talk deeply about what we mean when we urge
Black women and men to "get it together."

CW I think again that we have to keep in mind the larger
context of American society, which has historically expressed contempt for Black men and Black women. The very notion that Black
people are human beings is a new notion in Western Civilization
and is still not widely accepted in practice. And one of the consequences of this pernicious idea is that it is very difficult for Black
men and women to remain attuned to each other's humanity, so
when bell talks about Black women's agency and some of the
problems Black men have when asked to acknowledge Black
women's humanity, it must be remembered that this refusal to acknowledge one another's humanity is a reflection of the way we
are seen and treated in the larger society. And it's certainly not true
that White folks have a monopoly on human relationships. When
we talk about a crisis in Western Civilization, Black people are a
part of that civilization, even though we have been beneath it, our
backs serving as a foundation for the building of that civilization,
and we have to understand how it affects us so that we may remain
attuned to each other's humanity, so that the partnership that bell
talks about can take on real substance and content. I think partner-
ships between Black men and Black women can be made when
we learn how to be supportive and think in terms of critical affirmation.

bh Certainly, Black people have not talked enough about the
importance of constructing patterns of interaction that strengthen
our capacity to be affirming.

CW We need to affirm one another, support one another,
help, enable, equip, and empower one another to deal with the
present crisis, but it can't be uncritical, because if it's uncritical,
then we are again refusing to acknowledge other people's humanity. If we are serious about acknowledging and affirming other
people's humanity, then we are committed to trusting and believing that they are forever in process. Growth, development, maturation happens in stages. People grow, develop, and mature along
the lines in which they are taught. Disenabling critique and con-
temptuous feedback hinders.

bh We need to examine the function of critique in traditional Black communities. Often it does not serve as a constructive force. Like we have that popular slang word "dissin'," and we know that "dissin'" refers to a kind of disenabling contempt—when we "read" each other in ways that are so painful, so cruel, that the person can't get up from where you have knocked them down. Other destructive forces in our lives are envy and jealousy. These undermine our efforts to work for a collective good. Let me give a minor example. When I came in this morning I saw Cornel's latest book on the table. I immediately wondered why my book was not there and caught myself worrying about whether he was receiving some gesture of respect or recognition denied me. When he heard me say, "Where's my book?" he pointed to another table.

Often when people are suffering a legacy of deprivation, there is a sense that there are never enough goodies to go around, so that we must viciously compete with one another. Again this spirit of competition creates conflict and divisiveness. In a larger social context, competition between Black women and men has surfaced around the issue of whether Black female writers are receiving more attention than Black male writers. Rarely does anyone point to the reality that only a small minority of Black women writers are receiving public accolades. Yet the myth that Black women who succeed are taking something away from Black men continues to permeate Black psyches and inform how we as Black women and men respond to one another. Since capitalism is rooted in unequal distribution of resources, it is not surprising that we as Black women and men find ourselves in situations of competition and conflict.

CW I think part of the problem is deep down in our psyche we recognize that we live in such a conservative society, a society disproportionately shaped by business elites, a society in which corporate power influences are assuring that a certain group of people do get up higher.

bh Right, including some of you in this room.

CW And this is true not only between male and female relations but also Black and Brown relations, and Black and Red, and Black and Asian relations. We are struggling over crumbs because we know that the bigger part has been received by elites in corporate America. One half of one percent of America owns twenty-two percent of the wealth, one percent owns thirty-two percent, and the bottom forty-five percent of the population has two percent of the wealth. So, you end up with this kind of crabs-in-the-barrel mentality. When you see someone moving up, you immediately think they'll get a bigger cut in big-loaf corporate America, and you think that's something real because we're still shaped by the corporate ideology of the larger context.

bh Here at Yale, many of us are getting a slice of that miniloaf and yet are despairing. It was discouraging when I came here to teach and found in many Black people a quality of despair which is not unlike what we know is felt in "crack neighborhoods." I wanted to understand the connection between underclass Black despair and that of Black people here who have immediate and/or potential access to so much material privilege. This despair mirrors the spiritual crisis that is happening in our culture as a whole. Nihilism is everywhere. Some of this despair is rooted in a deep sense of loss. Many Black folks who have made it or are making it undergo an identity crisis. This is especially true for individual Black people working to assimilate into the "mainstream." Suddenly, they may feel panicked, alarmed by the knowledge that they do not understand their history, that life is without purpose and meaning. These feelings of alienation and estrangement create suffering. The suffering many Black people experience today is linked to the suffering of the past, to "historical memory." Attempts by Black people to understand that suffering, to come to terms with it, are the conditions which enable a work like Toni Morrison's *Beloved* to receive so much attention. To look back, not just to describe slavery but to try and reconstruct a psycho-social history of its impact has only recently been fully understood as a necessary stage in the process of collective Black self-recovery.

CW The spiritual crisis that has happened, especially among the well-to-do Blacks, has taken the form of the quest for therapeutic release. So that you can get very thin, flat, and one-dimensional forms of spirituality that are simply an attempt to sustain the well-to-do Black folks as they engage in their consumerism and privatism. The kind of spirituality we're talking about is not the kind that serves as an opium to help you justify and rationalize your own cynicism vis-à-vis the disadvantaged folk in our community. We could talk about churches and their present role in the crisis of America, religious faith as the American way of life, the gospel of health and wealth, helping the bruised psyches of the Black middle class make it through America. That's not the form of spirituality that we're talking about. We're talking about something deeper—you used to call it conversion—so that notions of service and risk and sacrifice once again become fundamental. It's very important, for example, that those of you who remember the days in which Black colleges were hegemonic among the Black elite remember them critically but also acknowledge that there was something positive going on there. What was going on was that you were told every Sunday, in chapel, that you had to give service to the race. Now it may have been a petty bourgeois form, but it created a moment of accountability, and with the erosion of the service ethic the very possibility of putting the needs of others alongside of one's own diminishes. In this syndrome, me-ness, selfishness, and egocentricity become more and more prominent, creating a spiritual crisis where you need more psychic opium to get you over.

bh We have experienced such a change in that communal ethic of service that was so necessary for survival in traditional Black communities. That ethic of service has been altered by shifting class relations. And even those Black folks who have little or no class mobility may buy into a bourgeois class sensibility; TV shows like *Dallas* and *Dynasty* teach ruling class ways of thinking and being to underclass poor people. A certain kind of bourgeois individualism of the mind prevails. It does not correspond to actual class reality or circumstances of deprivation. We need to remember the many economic structures and class politics that have led to a shift of priorities for "privileged" Blacks. Many privileged Black folks obsessed with living out a bourgeois dream of liberal individualistic success no longer feel as though they have any accountability in relation to the Black poor and underclass.

CW We're not talking about the narrow sense of guilt privileged Black people can feel, because guilt usually paralyzes action. What we're talking about is how one uses one's time and energy. We're talking about the ways in which the Black middle class, which is relatively privileged vis-à-vis the Black working class, working poor, and underclass, needs to acknowledge that along with that privilege goes responsibility. Somewhere I read that for those to whom much is given, much is required. And the question becomes, "How do we exercise that responsibility, given our privilege?" I don't think it's a credible notion to believe the Black middle class will give up on its material toys. No, the Black middle class will act like any other middle class in human history; it will attempt to maintain its privilege. There is something seductive about comfort and convenience. The Black middle class will not return to the ghetto, especially given the territorial struggles going on with gangs and so forth. Yet, how can we use what power we do have to be sure more resources are available to those who are disadvantaged? So the question becomes "How do we use our responsibility and privilege?" Because, after all, Black privilege is a result of Black struggle.

I think the point to make here is that there is a new day in Black America. It is the best of times and the worst of times in Black America. Political consciousness is escalating in Black America, among Black students, among Black workers, organized Black workers and trade unions. Increasingly we are seeing Black local leaders with vision. The Black church is on the move, Black popular music, political themes and motifs are on the move. So don't think in our critique we somehow ask you to succumb to a paralyzing pessimism. There are grounds for hope and when that corner is turned—and we don't know what particular catalytic event will serve as the take-off for it (just like we didn't know December 1955 would be the take-off)—but when it occurs we have got to be ready. The privileged Black folks can play a rather crucial role if we have a service ethic, if we want to get on board, if we want to be part of the progressive, prophetic bandwagon. And that is the question we will have to ask ourselves and each other.

bh We also need to remember that there is a joy in struggle. Recently, I was speaking on a panel at a conference with another Black woman from a privileged background. She mocked the notion of struggle. When she expressed, "I'm just tired of hearing about the importance of struggle; it doesn't interest me," the audience clapped. She saw struggle solely in negative terms, a perspective which led me to question whether she had ever taken part in any organized resistance movement. For if you have, you know that there is joy in struggle. Those of us who are old enough to remember segregated schools, the kind of political effort and sacrifice folks were making to ensure we would have full access to educational opportunities, surely remember the sense of fulfillment when goals that we struggled for were achieved. When we sang together "We shall overcome," there was a sense of victory, a sense of power that comes when we strive to be self-determining. When Malcolm X spoke about his journey to Mecca, the awareness he achieved, he gives expression to that joy that comes from struggling to grow. When Martin Luther King talked about having been to the mountain top, he was sharing with us that he arrived at a peak of critical awareness, and it gave him great joy. In our liberatory pedagogy, we must teach young Black folks to understand that struggle is process, that one moves from circumstances of difficulty and pain to awareness, joy, fulfillment. That the struggle to be critically conscious can be that movement which takes you to another level, that lifts you up, that makes you feel better. You feel good, you feel your life has meaning and purpose.

CW A rich life is fundamentally a life of serving others, a life of trying to leave the world a little better than you found it. That rich life comes into being in human relationships. This is true at the personal level. Those of you who have been in love know what I am talking about. It is also true at the organizational and communal level. It's difficult to find joy by yourself even if you have all the right toys. It's difficult. Just ask somebody who has got a lot of material possessions but doesn't have anybody to share them with. Now that's at the personal level. There is a political version of this. It has to do with what you see when you get up in the morning and look in the mirror and ask yourself whether you are simply wasting time on the planet or spending time in an enriching manner. We are talking fundamentally about the meaning of life and the place of struggle. bell talks about the significance of struggle and service. For those of us who are Christians there are certain theological foundations on which our commitment to serve is based. Christian life is understood to be a life of service. Even so, Christians have no monopoly on the joys that come from service and those of you who are part of secular culture can also enjoy this sense of enrichment. Islamic brothers and sisters share in a religious practice which also places emphasis on the importance of service. When we speak of commitment to a life of service we must also talk about the fact that such a commitment goes against the grain, especially the foundations of our society. To talk this way about service and struggle, we must also talk about strategies that will enable us to sustain this sensibility, this commitment.

bh When we talk about that which will sustain and nurture our spiritual growth as a people, we must once again talk about the importance of community. For one of the most vital ways we sustain ourselves is by building communities of resistance, places where we know we are not alone. In *Prophetic Fragments,* Cornel began his essay on Martin Luther King by quoting the lines of the spiritual, "He promised never to leave me, never to leave me alone." In Black spiritual tradition, the promise that we will not be alone cannot be heard as an affirmation of passivity. It does not mean we can sit around and wait for God to take care of business. We are not alone when we build community together. Certainly, there is a great feeling of community in this room today. And yet when I was here at Yale I felt that my labor was not appreciated. It was not clear that my work was having meaningful impact. Yet I feel that impact today. When I walked into the room a Black woman sister let me know how much my teaching and writing had helped her. There's more of the critical affirmation Cornel spoke of. That critical affirmation says, "Sister, what you're doing is uplifting me in some way." Often folk think that those folks who are spreading the message are so "together" that we do not need affirmation, critical dialogue about the impact of all that we teach and write about and how we live in the world.

CW It is important to note the degree to which Black people in particular, and progressive people in general, are alienated and estranged from communities that would sustain and support us. We are often homeless. Our struggles against a sense of nothingness and attempts to reduce us to nothing are ongoing. We confront regularly the question: "Where can I find a sense of home?" That sense of home can only be found in our construction of those communities of resistance bell talks about and the solidarity we can experience within them. Renewal comes through participating in community. That is the reason so many folks continue to go to church. In religious experience they find a sense of renewal, a sense of home. In community one can feel that we are moving forward, that struggle can be sustained. As we go forward as Black progressives, we must remember that community is not about homogeneity. Homogeneity is dogmatic imposition, pushing your way of life, your way of doing things onto somebody else. That is not what we mean by community. Dogmatic insistence that everybody think and act alike causes rifts among us, destroying the possibility of community. That sense of home that we are talking about and searching for is a place where we can find compassion, recognition of difference, of the importance of diversity, of our individual uniqueness.

bh When we evoke a sense of home as a place where we can renew ourselves, where we can know love and the sweet communion of shared spirit, I think it's important for us to remember that this location of well-being cannot exist in a context of sexist domination, in a setting where children are the objects of parental domination and abuse. On a fundamental level, when we talk about home, we must speak about the need to transform the African American home, so that there, in that domestic space, we can experience the renewal of political commitment to the Black liberation struggle. So that there in that domestic space we learn to serve and honor one another. If we look again at the civil rights movement, at the Black power movement, folks organized so much in homes. They were the places where folks got together to educate themselves for critical consciousness. That sense of community, cultivated and developed in the home, extended outward into a larger, more public context. As we talk about Black power in the 21st century, about political partnership between Black women and men, we must talk about transforming our notions of how and why we bond. In *Beloved,* Toni Morrison offers a paradigm for relationships between Black men and women. Sixo describes his love for Thirty-Mile Woman, declaring, "She is a friend of mind. She gather me, man. The pieces I am, she gather them and give them back to me in all the right order. It's good, you know, when you got a woman who is a friend of your mind." In this passage, Morrison evokes a notion of bonding that may be rooted in passion, desire, even romantic love, but the point of connection between Black women and men is that space of recognition and understanding, where we know one another so well, our histories, that we can take the bits and pieces, the fragments of who we are, and put them back together, re-member them. It is this joy of intellectual bonding, of working together to create liberatory theory and analysis that Black women and men can give one another, that Cornel and I give to each other. We are friends of one another's mind. We find a home with one another. It is that joy in community we celebrate and share with you this morning.

2

Introduction to Cornel West

Praxis is a specific kind of obedience that organizes itself around a social theory of reality in order to implement in the society the freedom, inherent in faith. If faith is the belief that God created all for freedom, then praxis is the social theory used to analyze what must be done for the historical realization of freedom. To sing about freedom and to pray for its coming is not enough. Freedom must be actualized in history by oppressed peoples who accept the intellectual challenge to analyze the world for the purpose of changing it.

James Cone
Speaking the Truth

Walking in the wet streets of New York after we had talked together for hours, Cornel West paused to rap with a brother in a wheelchair, handing over a few dollars. Standing at a distance observing them, Cornel in his three-piece suit, meticulously shined shoes, the brother wearing a mix-match of old clothes, his legs covered by a tattered blanket, I listened as they talked about how the struggle has changed since "We lost Malcolm." Cornel nods his head as the brother says, "We need more Malcolms." They stand talking in the wet, Cornel nodding his head, commenting. As we walk away, the brother calls out, "You're as good as Malcolm." Cornel responds, "I wish. I just do the best I can." There is a modesty, a humility in Cornel West's voice that folks attending his lectures at Harvard, Yale, Princeton, and countless other colleges and universities may never hear. The intimacy of this dialogue between an extremely privileged Black man and one of the underclass is in part a reflection of West's profound understanding of the way politics of race, class, and gender determine the fate of Black men, and his ongoing commitment to eradicating structures of domination that create and maintain suffering. Ultimately, it is his deep love of Black culture and Black people that surfaces in the night air; the solidarity expressed is real, the sense of brotherhood, the knowledge that he must sustain his connection to the oppressed as it is that bond which brings him to the deepest level of history.

A child of the Fifties, Cornel did undergraduate work at Harvard, finishing his graduate degree at Princeton. Speaking autobiographically in the preface to his first book, *Prophesy Deliverance! An Afro-American Revolutionary Christianity,* West asserts: "The particular perspective presented in this book bears the indelible stamp of my own existential, intellectual, and political story. I was nurtured in the bosom of a loving Black family and church (Shiloh Baptist Church in Sacramento California) and I remain committed to the prophetic Christian gospel. I am the product of an Ivy League education which reinforced my unfathomable interest in and unquenchable curiosity about the Western philosophical tradition, American culture, and Afro-American history and I have an affinity to a philosophical version of American pragmatism. Lastly, I was politically awakened by the crypto-Marxism of the Black Panther Party and schooled in the Hegelian Marxism of Georg Lukacs and the Frankfurt school…and I possess an abiding allegiance to progressive Marxist social analysis and political praxis." Cornel wrote these words in 1982, yet their testimony stands. Reviewing this book in 1983, M. Shawn Copeland identified it as "one of the most important and sophisticated extended statements in the field of Black Religious Studies in recent years." *Prophesy Deliverance!* explored the development of African American critical thought, emphasizing the impact of evangelical prophetic Christianity and American pragmatism. Significantly, West called attention to the way in which prophetic Christianity was rooted in the belief that every individual irrespective of race, class, gender, or nationality should have the opportunity of self-realization and self-fulfillment. This early work simply laid the groundwork for West's continual critical exploration of the links between African American religious experience, prophetic Christianity, and the struggle for Black liberation that is rooted in a pragmatic revolutionary Left praxis. Cornel West is unique among Black intellectuals in that he has always courageously identified himself with Marxist social analysis, and socialist political movement in the United States.

Currently professor of religion and director of African American studies at Princeton University, West has taught at Union Theological Seminary and at the Yale Divinity School. Politically active as a leader of Democratic Socialists of America, he spreads the message of Left commitment to radical social change throughout the world. Cornel and I first met at the annual Socialist Scholars Conference. Later, I would come to know him best during the years when we were colleagues at Yale University. There he was in constant demand. Students eager to work with him came from diverse disciplines. To students concerned with radical social change, who longed to link the knowledge they were learning with a lived political practice, he was a beacon, a messenger showing the way. Attending his course on Afro-American Critical Thought students grappled with the relevance of Marxism to Black life, examined the connections between Black spirituality and Black liberation struggles, looked at questions of gender, critiqued sexism, studied Black feminist thought. His classroom was a space for rigorous intellectual challenge and debate; it was in those days the place to be. Unlike many other Black intellectuals in the academy, Cornel West offered a Left standpoint, let students know that theory was a form of practice. He gave them the tools to think critically and analytically about African American experience, providing a liberatory pedagogy that was empowering and enabling. Speaking at high schools, churches, at DSA meetings, Cornel does not limit himself to teaching in the academy, he goes wherever he is called. At the community based African American Cultural Center in West Los Angeles, he is one of the Black leaders whose face adorns the wall, with Malcolm, Martin, Angela Davis, and a host of others.

The range of Cornel West's intellectual concerns are most visible in his second book *Prophetic Fragments*, a collection of essays published by Africa World Press in 1988. Theorist of postmodernism, philosopher, theologian, cultural critic, Cornel writes on multiple subjects from Martin Luther King to Marvin Gaye, from genealogy of racism to reconstructing the American Left. Continually focused on the concerns of African Americans both cultural and political, he analyzes the Jesse Jackson campaign, looks at Black theology of liberation as critique of capitalist civilization. There are few intellectuals in the United States able to speak in an informed way about so many subjects, whose influence reaches far beyond the academy. Indeed, for many Black Americans, watching Cornel West on the Bill Moyers show broadcast from Riverside Church was a major cultural event signifying a change in who is allowed to speak for and about Black experience.

No wonder, then, that fellow philosopher K. Anthony Appiah, reviewing Cornel West's book *The American Evasion of Philosophy: A Genealogy of Pragmatism,* in *The Nation* tells readers that West "may well be the pre-eminent African American intellectual of our generation." Appiah continues: "Highly influential as a theorist of postmodernism, West bridges cultural theory and the Black community, inserting the issue of the progressive potential of the Black church, for example, into debates about the politics of postmodernity, while transforming discussions in the Black community with his sharp sense of the relevance of Christianity and socialism, his work displays an inexhaustible appetite for ideas and a compelling moral vision." *The American Evasion of Philosophy* is difficult reading, yet worth the effort. It is, as Appiah states, "a powerful call for philosophy to play its role in building a radical democracy in alliance with the wretched of the earth."

Knowing that many folks, especially poor Black people, are not literate in this society, that the struggle for literacy is part of the political project he advocates, as a lay preacher West is able to speak with diverse audiences. Speaking from multiple locations, his work helps shape disciplinary concerns in a wide range of academic arenas. Recently, *The Journal of Negro Education* , a Howard University quarterly review of issues relevant to the education of Black people, included an essay, "Leadership and a Critical Pedagogy of Race." Authors, Peter McLaren and Michael Dantley critically examine West's work because it "offers an empowering pedagogical alternative for leaders in education." Insisting that a critical pedagogy of race must articulate the collective African American experience, McLaren and Dantley call attention to the way West's work offers direction to those non-Black groups who want to be allies in struggle. Learning from his analysis of African American prophetic traditions, they conclude: "Efforts to silence or marginalize the generative themes and social practice of the African American prophetic tradition or to obstruct their national progression negate the very crux of the African American struggle. Unless we educators wish to buttress the very ideologies that are undermined by an emergent African American critical consciousness and become exegetes of political impotence, we must develop a mode of sounding reality that speaks directly to the politics of difference." Always willing to exchange ideas with diverse groups, West never compromises his commitment to an intellectual and political practice that addresses the concerns of the Black masses.

More than most contemporary Black intellectuals, West works to link academic concerns with larger political issues. If they say of West that he is "a race man" they mean that he does not simply talk about race or commodify it for a White audience but that he actively works to improve the lot of all Black people. His provocative essay "Minority Discourse and the Pitfalls of Canon Formation," published in *The Yale Journal of Criticism,* urged scholars and cultural critics who focus primarily on studying political conflict and struggle as it is delineated in texts to "relate such conflict and struggle to larger institutional and structural battles occurring in and across societies, cultures, and economies." Particularly critical of Black intellectuals who do not assume leadership roles in relation to Black community, in the essays "The Dilemma of the Black Intellectual" and "The Crisis of Black Leadership," West challenges Black critical thinkers to candidly acknowledge that there is a crisis, a vacuum of leadership. With outspoken candor he asserts: "We need national forums to reflect, discuss, and plan how best to respond. It is neither a matter of a new Messiah figure emerging, nor of another organization appearing on the scene. Rather, it is a matter of grasping the structural and institutional processes that have disfigured, deformed, and devastated Black America such that the resources for collective and critical consciousness, moral commitment and courageous engagement are vastly underdeveloped. We need serious strategic and tactical thinking about how to create new models of leadership and forge the kind of persons to actualize these models. These models must not only question our silent assumptions about Black leadership such as the notion that Black leaders are always middle class but also force us to interrogate iconic figures of the past. This includes questioning King's sexism and homophobia and the relatively undemocratic character of his organization, and Malcolm's silence in the vicious role of priestly versions of Islam in the modern world." Critically affirming the power of iconic Black leaders, West also emphasizes the importance of caring critique, so that we learn from past struggles how to strengthen and renew ourselves for the future.

Contrary to notions that a prophet will not be recognized among his or her own community, African Americans struggling to make sense of the crisis we are facing as a people, economic as-

sault, genocidal attacks, resurgence of overt racism and White supremacy, widespread drug addiction, and pervasive despair, are
turning to intellectuals, to folks like Cornel West, for insight and
guidance. Throughout his career, the word "prophetic" has
emerged as that expression which best names both West's intellectual project, his spiritual commitment, and his revolutionary political agenda. Letting his light shine, West awakens us from the
slumber of indifference, narcissism, obsession with material success, and calls us as in prophetic scripture, to "not be conformed to
this world, but be transformed by the renewing of our minds." It is
a call that urges African Americans to think critically so that we
may live differently, to act wisely so that we may be politically prepared to create the revolutionary future.

3

Cornel West Interviewed by bell hooks

Death is always close by. And what's important is not to know if you can avoid it, but to know that you have done the most possible to realize your ideas.

Frantz Fanon
Letter December, 1961

bh Cornel, in your essay "The Dilemma of the Black Intellectual," you talk about your intellectual development. Could you talk a little bit about that now? Why did you become an intellectual? What was the impetus to become an intellectual, an academic?

CW There were intrinsic reasons and extrinsic reasons. Intrinsically, it is a wonderful way to live one's life. I receive tremendous joy and pleasure from reading books and conversing about ideas.

Extrinsic reasons have to do with the instrumental value of ideas, the fact that ideas are forms of power, and because I understood myself primarily as an intellectual freedom fighter in the Black Christian tradition, I understood ideas as not only sources of pleasure but also sources of power. Ideas can be used in such a way that it promotes the enhancement and advancement of poor people in general, and Black people in particular.

bh Where does this radical understanding of what it means to be an intellectual come from? One is not born with the sense of what an intellectual is.

CW In my own case, it's a matter of a particular tradition that I'm part of, a prophetic Christian tradition in the Black community, and Black preachers have often served as models for me to the degree to which they used their vision and their analysis and their example as a way of affirming the humanity of Black people. And as an intellectual, I actually use this model within the sphere of ideas.

bh You were an athlete in your youth, yet when I think of athletes who have focused on intellectual development, I think of someone like Kareem Abdul Jabbar. And if one reads his 1985 autobiography, we see how much he works to become a man of ideas, a man who thinks critically. Could you talk a little bit about the connection between your early experience as an athlete and how you went on to pursue a life of the mind when so many Black athletes are not encouraged to do so?

CW That is a very interesting question, because on the one hand, athletics is so very important to the Black community, usually as a form of male bonding, and sometimes woman bonding.

In my own case, athletics was a source of fun and joy, and also a means to create character and integrity out of discipline, out of working with others, out of pursuing a goal and trying to achieve it. So, for me, the application of discipline to the life of the mind was in part based on my athletic career, athletic involvement, athletic activities.

At the same time, I would want to argue that it is primarily among athletes that you get high levels of discipline, more discipline than most people in society on the whole exercise.

Now, to the degree to which they are able to use that discipline as a basis for critical engagement, critical consciousness, like, let's say, an Abdul Jabbar, does not occur as much as one would like.

bh Well, given that struggle on your part to link life of the mind with a radical political perspective, what do you think about the role of contemporary Black intellectuals?

CW I wish that contemporary Black intellectuals were more visible. I wish that they were more critical and self-critical. I wish that what they had to say had more visibility in the Black community as opposed to, let's say, the Black politicians and the Black entertainers, who I think are oftentimes overexposed.

bh Are there that many of us (Black intellectuals)?

CW Yes, I think there are a significant number. We need more, but there are a significant number. But most Black intellectuals are still caught in academic cocoons with very little sense of outreach to or exposure to the larger public sphere of the Black community or larger society.

bh That is what I was going to ask you, if you think there is a difference between being an academic and an intellectual. Because, when I think of Black intellectual traditions that an Anna Julia Cooper or W.E.B. DuBois came out of, it is a tradition based on the analysis of specific political cultures within a global context. Yet, today's specialized professional training of academics often doesn't promote that kind of thinking.

CW I think that's true. There is a fundamental difference between an academic and an intellectual. An academic usually engages in rather important yet still narrow scholarly work, whereas an intellectual is engaged in the public issues that affect large numbers of people in a critical manner.

Yet, I would still want to suggest that those Black intellectuals who are in the academy ought to have much more visibility. That's why it is so very good to have an interview such as this.

bh One of the things I find so striking about this interview is having two Black intellectuals engage in public dialogue with one another. We often are talking to the White majority. For example, in your recent televised discussion with Bill Moyers, in which it was exciting for us to see your intellectual presence, we still reproduce this sense of White people coming to Black intellectuals to be informed, which is very different from us talking with one another about our situation as Black people. This we have not done enough.

CW That is very true.

bh Can we be oppositional? Are we oppositional as Black intellectuals, and can we be in the academy?

CW Oh, very much so. I think you and I are oppositional. The crucial question remains—is our opposition effective? And I would say at this point no. Opposition, meaning progressive critique and progressive resistance, is not very effective these days, even though many of us are going to continue bringing critique to bear on this society in light of those who suffer and bear the social cost until we die. What we need presently is to come up with a way of making links with those other persons in the larger Black and White progressive communities who are investing their time and energies to create larger spaces for social change. And here,

Black intellectuals in particular, but progressive intellectuals as a whole, have yet to be able to come up with strategies and programs to form those kinds of links.

bh You suggested in "The Dilemma of the Black Intellectual" that Black intellectuals must accentuate the practical dimension of their work. Can you give some example of this?

CW One way of talking about this is by defining what I call a critical organic catalyst, an intellectual who is rooted in a particular indigenous tradition in the Black community, a prophetic Black preacher would be a good example. A Carolyn Knight [sic] for example, who pastors here in Harlem, is very much in her activities and interests an organic intellectual. She is rooted in the Black community in Philadelphia Baptist Church and at the same time she's engaged in the life of the mind, writing, reading, and so forth. And there are hundreds of others. These individuals serve to me as both exemplars as well as signs of hope.

bh Growing up, the way I knew there even was such a thing as a Black intellectual before I was, you know, in—high school, was hearing Black preachers come to our church, many of whom were studying and teaching in divinity schools in Tennessee. As a critical thinker with a graduate degree, our pastor Dr. A.R. Lasley invited celebrated scholars like Kelly Miller Smith to our church.

CW Yes, he was a great preacher and a learned man.

bh And he was one of the first preachers who came to our church and linked a criticism of politics with our Black spiritual tradition, and that was very, very, poignant to me, because here were these Black theological scholars bringing a different kind of analysis to bear on Christian understanding. And I was very privileged to be raised in that church and also why I see the roots of my intellectualism as emerging from the traditional Southern Black Baptist Church.

CW And I don't want to suggest by any means that the church is the only avenue. We are just talking about our own personal experiences. I don't think it's an accident that the prophetic church tradition, with all of its problems and with all its great insights, continues to produce persons like ourselves, who are deeply dedicated to the life of the mind while at the same time deeply devoted to the struggle for freedom.

bh We were colleagues at Yale, me as professor in the English Department and Afro-American Studies, you at Yale Divinity School. What inspired your greater involvement in African American studies after Yale?

CW Ruth Simmons, who is now vice Provost at Princeton, suggested that I apply for the Director of Afro-American Studies at Princeton. My major motivation had to do with being able to work with the great Toni Morrison. I had left Yale and returned to Union Seminary. I would probably be there today, still teaching philosophy, if Toni had not been at Princeton. Once that opportunity presented itself, I decided instantly and am glad I did.

I am now strategically and institutionally linked to Afro-American studies, which is different from my previous positions, although there is a continuity between my work when I was there in New Haven and my work here at Princeton, since much of what I write really does focus on the various dimensions and aspects of Afro-American experience .

bh Well, I think one of the things that you emphasized in a number of your essays on Black intellectuality is the need for us to be involved both in collective work and in ongoing intellectual dialogue with one another. As a young graduate student who wrote her dissertation on Toni Morrison, I can certainly understand the significance of intellectual fellowship with her. I think one of the exciting movements happening now among Black critical thinkers is that we are developing the kind of traditions where we can look to one another for both intellectual camaraderie and ongoing critical intellectual feedback.

CW I agree.

bh Why do you think universities like Princeton, Duke, Harvard, and any number of schools we could name which were once completely uninterested in creating a diverse academic environment, are now engaged in promoting Black studies? What's their agenda?

CW Well, we live in a very different world now. We saw the collapse of Europe in 1945. We are seeing the decline of the American empire in the 1990's. We've seen the dissolution of the Soviet empire in the latter part of the 1980's. It's a very different world— which means then that the struggles, the sufferings, and the contributions of those who were once on the underside of these worlds: Third World people—Asia, Africa, and Latin America—are emerging now, becoming tremendous powers, culturally, intellectually, artistically, even more so than politically and economically. And so these universities, which are in many ways repositories of the different kinds of shifts going on in the world as expressed intellectually, must indeed respond.

bh In some ways, that takes me back to comments we made about whether we can be oppositional in the academy. Certainly, one of the most exciting experiences I've had as a professor was teaching at Yale. And partially it was exciting because of the eagerness on the part of students of all ethnicities to engage in what Foucault has called, "the insurrection of subjugated knowledges." To teach a course on Black women writers and have hundreds of the students signing up, that let's you know that there has been a transformation in the academy.

CW That's exactly right. And I think this hunger and thirst that you talk about has much to do with not only the changing forces in the world, changing contexts in the world. We saw it in music in the 1960's, where there's been a kind of Afro-Americanization of White youth, and that's going on now internationally. And that in some ways prefigures what is further down the road when it comes to intellectual focus on issues of race and "otherness".

bh Well, can you speak about that? I know one of the things that I'm confronting increasingly as a Black academic is that often our Black Studies classes are peopled predominantly by White students and students of diverse ethnicities—more Asian students from all Asian ethnicities, more Chicanos, and more Puerto Ricans, et cetera. What does this mean for the future of Black studies? Does it mean that the nature of the discipline is changing? Or are we simply being more inclusive?

CW No, I think it's a good sign. Afro-American Studies was never meant to be solely for Afro-Americans. It was meant to try to redefine what it means to be human, what it means to be modern, what it means to be American, because people of African descent in this country are profoundly human, profoundly modern, profoundly American. And so to the degree to which they can see the riches that we have to offer as well as see our shortcomings, is the degree to which they can more fully understand the modern and what modernity is all about, and more fully understand the American experience,

bh At a conference sponsored by Men Stopping Violence and the National Organization for Men Against Sexism, I tried to emphasize that all groups of men in the United States can understand masculinity better by understanding Black masculinity, rather than constituting Black masculinity as "other." Certainly, White men might learn more about the production of what it is to be men by studying about Black men and how Black men experience life in this society. It seems to me that in our liberatory pedagogies, we bring that kind of analysis of subjectivity to bear which says that studying "the other" is not the goal, the goal is learning about some aspect of who you are.

CW That's precisely right. Ralph Ellison used to make that point with great insight and profundity. And to the degree to which not just Americans, but modern persons accept that to understand themselves they must understand the Afro-American experience is the degree to which Afro-American Studies is, in part, successful.

bh Cornel, you are unique in that you come to Black Studies from Philosophy. Many of the traditional movers and shakers in Black Studies have been historians, literary critics, social scientists. Do you bring a different approach?

CW By being trained in philosophy?

bh Yes.

CW I think so. As a philosopher, I'm fundamentally concerned with how we confront death, dread, despair, disappointment, and disease. These are existential issues. And sociologists, economists, social scientists, they are not primarily concerned with how individuals confront their inevitable doom, their inescapable extinction. So that there is a sensibility I, and other philosophers, bring to issues of meaning and value that other intellectuals may not have.

bh That focus on meaning and values is truly evident in your book, *The American Evasion of Philosophy,* which explores the importance of American pragmatism.

Now this book is in many ways a difficult book to read, a rigorous book. And I think people should approach it with that understanding, because certainly the earlier works, *Prophesy Deliverance: Afro-American Revolutionary Christianity,* that came out in 1982, and then *Prophetic Fragments,* in 1988 are much more solidly rooted in a focus on Black culture and Black tradition. Many Black readers would come to these books with some awareness of the fundamental ideas you are talking about—that might not be the case with the book on American pragmatism. What does prophetic pragmatism mean? What are its implications for Black community?

CW It helps us to understand that we have to interpret both American civilization and the modern West from our vantage point. This is what *The American Evasion of Philosophy* actually is, an interpretation of the emergence, the sustenance, and the decline of American civilization from the vantage point of an African-American. It means then we have to have a cosmopolitan orientation, even though it is rooted in the fundamental concern with the plight and predicament of African Americans.

Now, what the text attempts to do is to argue that there are fundamental themes like experimentation and improvisation that can be found in the works of Ralph Waldo Emerson, for example, that are thoroughly continuous with the great art form that Afro-Americans have given the modern world, which is jazz. And therefore to talk about America is to talk about improvisation and experimentation, and therefore to talk about Emerson and Louis Armstrong in the same breath.

bh That is why I was very moved by our talking about prophetic pragmatism as "a form of Third Wave Left Romanticism," which you said, "tempers its utopian impulse with the profound sense of the tragic character of life in history."

One of the things that seemed to me that you were trying to do in giving us this philosophical framework is to say that Black people must theorize our experience in such a way that we come to understand our tragedies beyond solely the emotionally felt experience of that tragedy.

CW And the fact that when you look closely at jazz, or the blues, for example, we see a sense of the tragic, a profound sense of the tragic linked to human agency. So that it does not wallow in a cynicism or a paralyzing pessimism, but it also is realistic enough not to project excessive utopia. It's a matter of responding in an improvisational, undogmatic, creative way to circumstances, in such a way that people still survive and thrive. This is a great tradition intellectually, in fact, it has had tremendous impact on the way in which Americans as a whole respond to the human condition, respond to their circumstances.

bh One unique aspect of your discussion with Bill Moyers was that you talked about "the vocation of the intellectual as trying to allow suffering to speak." How do we transform the meaninglessness that people feel into an effective form of struggle? It seems to me that right there, when Black intellectuals start trying to answer that question, we begin the process of oppositionality both in action, practice, and theory.

CW That's right.

bh Could you say a little bit about the significance of theory?

CW Yes. Theory ought not to be a fetish. It does not have magical powers of its own. On the other hand, theory is inescapable because it is an indispensable weapon in struggle, and it is an indispensable weapon in struggle because it provides certain kinds of understanding, certain kinds of illumination, certain kinds of insights that are requisite if we are to act effectively.

For example, the Marxist tradition has always meant much to me because of its notion of commodification, and the degree to which market forces have so fundamentally not only shaped our economy, but the way in which we understand value and use.

And so to talk about multi-national corporations on the one hand, and talk about advertising on the other, are indispensable ways of understanding the modern world and thereby indispensable ways of trying to locate and situate Black people and give us some reasons for why we are catching so much hell.

bh Part of the contemporary project for the oppositional Black intellectual is to address the significance of theory to our revisioning of Black liberation struggle, in our attempts to address both the crisis of Black people and the crisis that we're having in the culture as a whole.

That brings us to the critical issue of what place does the theorizing of White, Euro-centric intellectuals have for Black people? I read Terry Eagleton's book, *The Significance of Theory,* and what I liked very much about his particular essay on theory was that he tried to talk about how everyone uses theory in their practical daily life, which is certainly what I've tried to stress in my work, particularly when speaking to Black students who are questioning the significance of theory. What do you think about the fact that many of us are influenced these days by European theorists Michel Foucault, Julia Kristeva, Derrida, Lacan, and Third World, non-Black theorists like Edward Said, Gayatri Spivak, Homi Bhaba? What do those intellectuals outside Black experience have to teach us, say to us, that can in some way illuminate and enhance that struggle?

CW To be intellectual, no matter what color, means that one is going to be deeply influenced by other intellectuals of a variety of different colors. When it comes to Black intellectuals, we have to, on the one hand, be very open to insights from wherever they come. On the other hand, we must filter it in such a way that we never lose sight of what some of the silences are in the work of White theorists, especially as those silences relate to issues of class, gender, race, and empire. Why? Because class, gender, race, and empire are fundamental categories which Black intellectuals must use in order to understand the predicament of Black people. So there is, I would say, a selective significance of White intellectuals to the critical development of Black intellectuals.

bh Concurrently, increasingly what we are seeing is that more and more White intellectuals, are making Black culture and Black experience the subject of their intellectual and discursive practices. What do you think about that? Are these people our allies? Are we developing coalitions? Or are we being appropriated yet again?

CW There is something positive and something negative here. Look at the work of Eugene Genovese, a very important scholar on the subject of slavery. He is not always right but often very illuminating. He has made a great contribution, yet at the same time, one recognizes that White scholars are bringing certain baggage with them when they look at Black culture, no matter how subtle and sophisticated the formulations. Therefore, we must always be on guard to bring critique to bear on the baggage that they bring, even when that baggage provides certain insights.

bh Talk about it, Cornel.

CW So it's a positive and a negative thing. The thing we can't do is remain insular and think that we have a monopoly on how to understand ourselves. Because that is not the case at all. But, we must be critical across the board.

bh As long as we, Black academics and intellectuals, are doing work within the context of White supremacy, often what happens is that White theorists draw upon our work and our ideas, and get forms of recognition that are denied Black thinkers. The reality of appropriation has produced a real tension between many Black academics and those White scholars and colleagues who want to talk with us. Often Black scholars, especially feminist thinkers, tell me they fear ideas will be "ripped off" and they'll (White scholars) get the credit. Black folks are willing to share ideas, but there is a feeling now that a White academic might take your idea, write about it, and you'll never be cited. This is upsetting many Black scholars.

CW It is the Elvis Presley syndrome applied to the academic terrain. Internal dynamics of power make it very difficult for credits to be given where they are due, when that credit should be given to an individual who comes from a marginal, subordinated group within this country. It has to do with who has access to the legitimate and prestigious journals, who has access to the publishing houses, and so on. We have seen this phenomenon historically, and the best that we can do to fight against it is to either establish our own institutional networks that would give our texts visibility, or simply continue to bring critique to bear on the manipulation and the cooptation that goes on in the mainstream.

bh We also have to be willing to confront, in a positive way, those of our White colleagues who, in fact, see themselves as our allies. I once experienced a White woman scholar, whom I respect, give a talk where I felt that, in fact, she was laying out my own analytical and theoretical framework from *Ain't I a Woman,* and getting credit. So I went to her and said I really felt that what I was hearing was my work without...

CW Acknowledgement.

bh Acknowledgement. And she, being a comrade in struggle, told me she would go back and read my work to see if she had, in fact, unwittingly taken ideas from me without citing them as mine. So I don't think we should always assume a negative intentionality. We all read things and pick up things where we don't always remember the source it came from, and within a racist context, well, White people are accustomed to taking the labor of Black people for granted. We have to see that the same thing can happen with intellectual labor, so that sometimes confronting that situation in a positive way can make for a meaningful critical intervention.

CW I absolutely agree.

bh Another thing that makes you unusual as a head of Black Studies is being both a scholar in a highly traditional discipline like philosophy and your unique and profound engagement with popular culture. You write about music and art—can you speak about how you think cultural studies is linked to Black studies?

CW That is a very difficult question. Let me say a few things about it. First, I focus on popular culture because I focus on those areas where Black humanity is most powerfully expressed, where Black people have been able to articulate their sense of the world in a profound manner. And I see this primarily in popular culture.

Why not in high brow culture? Because the access has been so difficult. Why not in more academic forms? Because academic exclusion has been the rule for so long for large numbers of Black people that Black culture, for me, becomes a search for where Black people have left their imprint and fundamentally made a difference in terms of how certain art forms are understood. This is currently in popular culture. And it has been primarily in music, religion, visual arts, and fashion.

bh Don't you also think that those of us writing about popular culture are regarded with skepticism by traditional Black academics who have been more engaged with "high culture"? Don't those Black academics look at someone like you with skepticism, in the same way that more conservative White colleagues might look at you and say, you know, he's not really a philosopher; a real philosopher wouldn't be so interested in popular culture.

CW I think you are correct. What you have, on the one hand, is Black scholars, who are deeply preoccupied with receiving respect from their White peers, trying to resist all Black stereotypes. And, in many instances, running from some of the riches of Black culture in order to convince their White peers that they are not a part, in any way, of what has been so very important to Black people, Black music, Black speech, and Black religion.

It is interesting that the history of Black Studies in the United States has been one in which Black religion and music has played a very, very small role. Even though Black religion and music plays a fundamental role in the history of Black people. This has to do not only with the secular orientation of Black intellectuals, but because so many Black intellectuals believe that any association with Black religion makes them look bad in light of the secular orientations of their White colleagues. So they run away from it. It seems to me that what we have to do is undermine all stereotypes while embracing what have been some of the very rich insights and contributions of the Black folk, intellectually, politically, and culturally.

bh The role of poetry in traditional Black community is a prime example of that. So many of us came to performance art, to public speaking from both the Black Church and Black high schools under segregation.

CW Right. Right.

bh We also forget that in the 19th century there was a tremendous emphasis on the oratory. And for a lot of Black people that carried over and informed 20th century construction of Black culture.

I was raised in a working class Black family where, when the lights went out and the candles were lit, my folks would say get up and entertain us. Recite a poem.

CW I want to argue that music and rhetorical practices, especially Black preaching practices, have been the two major traditions owing to the exclusion of Black people in other spheres, even though many of us venture in those fields.

bh You often say that U.S. mass culture is disproportionately influenced by Black culture. I think the critical question to ask is whether or not that influence is oppositional. Does Black culture radicalize White American culture, Asian American culture, the culture of other ethnic groups?

CW It is oppositional, but there are different levels of oppositionality. There's what we call "thin" opposition, and then there's "thick" opposition. Thin opposition is a critique of American society that does not talk about the need for a redistribution of wealth, resources, and power. Thick opposition is an attempt to call into question the prevailing maldistribution of wealth in this society. Thin opposition is important, but it is not sufficient. And Black cultural influence has played a role in that thin opposition. Just affirming the humanity of Black people in America is still, in many instances, a subversive act. Yet, "thick" opposition is rarely put forward openly in Black culture.

bh Absolutely. I was giving a talk and speaking about representations of Black athletes in advertising culture, giving the critical read on that Hanes commercial with Michael Jordan and other products which commodify Black images, when a young White man spoke up about the image of Black athletes on cereal boxes, saying it was the first time in his life he felt he wanted to be a Black man. And, you know, the audience sneered, but I thought he had made a profound point, because for him to see this image as valuable, legitimate, and worthwhile put it in a more humanizing light, meaning he could potentially be close to this image, an act which might be subversive, threatening even to White supremacy. This is why critical readings of popular culture are so important. Critiquing representations, we understand more fully the subtleties between subject and object and their concomitant power dynamics at a given historical moment.

CW That's exactly right.

bh Critically reading of the Hanes commercial which featured Michael Jordan, I talked about how I experienced it as a Black woman. On one hand, as positive because we so rarely see the Black male body represented as positive sex symbol on national television. On the other hand, one could also critically examine how certain aspects of the representation were annihilating to Black male sexual presence.

CW A dialectical reading, where you accent the positive as well as the negative, but you acknowledge the degree to which it is responding to a particular context, is necessary. And that context will change in light of the positive contribution made within a response. And so the context is forever changing, but you highlight both good and bad, both positive and negative.

bh Let's return to the issue of whether Black culture radicalizes the culture as a whole, particularly White America. I was thinking, for example, of our solidarity with Black Caribbean culture and of reggae and rap as two forms of diasporic popular music that offer political messages. I used to wonder what are people thinking, what are White people thinking, as they listen to the lyrics of Third World singing, lyrics like "Who put the hammer and the hoe in the hands of the poor, why, tell me why, do the rich keep crying for more? Because some us ain't got no freedom."

CW Yes, but again, when I make the distinction between thin opposition and thick, that thin opposition is primarily a form of opposition that works on everyday practices at the cultural level. Cultural productions by Black people, like rap, are, in some instances, subversive, but at the same time they do not speak to the more fundamental issue of the maldistribution of power, wealth, and resources in this society. When you get something like reggae and rap, culturally, they function in a thin oppositional mode. They make gestures towards thick opposition—redistribution of wealth, but there is no translation of reggae or rap into a political movement.

bh Could there be?

CW Well, that's a good question. The best examples we have are contemporary social movements, feminist movements in the 70s and 80s, Civil Rights movement in the 50s and 60s, and Black Power movements in the 60s and 70s. These are the significant social movements in which Bernice Reagan and a whole host of other cultural workers played an important role. But it wasn't the translation of the music into politics that these movements represented. Rather, it was a fusion of musicians, cultural workers, writers, poets, as part of a larger movement. So I wouldn't suggest that a translation could take place from music to political action. It doesn't occur that simply.

bh When I first began to really listen to the music of John Coltrane, or to a Don Cherry or Cecil Taylor, I found out how many Black jazz musicians were interested in Eastern thought and Eastern religions, and somehow knowing that these cultural icons were exploring cultural and religious pluralism opened up for me the possibility of thinking about life in new ways. This also helped me to think about the construction of identity in relation to radical politics, precisely because these icons bring us a potential location for politicization when we move from listening to their music to learning about their lives. Unfortunately, so many of them do not engage in the disciplined and rigorous critical thinking which would make them both musical and political mentors.

Again, that is why I say Kareem Abdul Jabbar is important. In his first autobiography, he really does emphasize how deeply he was thinking about the politics of Blackness and race in the United States. As a Black Catholic who was raised to think in certain kinds of ways about identity, about race, about gender. Of course, he doesn't problematize gender as much as we would like. Certainly when I was in high school what was important about Kareem was that he was portrayed in the media as trying to think critically about issues, not simply passively absorbing them.

CW And before him Muhammad Ali was doing the same thing.

bh Absolutely. Ali was the precursor. But I think that because Kareem was situated at UCLA and was thinking about studying Arabic, his actions implied that it is not enough to simply convert to Islam without understanding something about the practice. That seems to me to be an arena where, when we have more fully radicalized political cultural icons, cultural production can be a catalyst for the development of political critical consciousness.

CW Well, I'll tell you why I highlight Muhammad Ali here, what we saw there, especially given the influence of Malcolm X, was the example of a Black person, in his case, a Black man, who was free from fear and failure. Fear and failure haunt Black people every minute of their lives.

bh Yes, absolutely.

CW Black people rarely get free from their fear of the White gaze, the fear of Black put-down, the fear of stepping out on their own and being independent. There is a fear of failure deeply ingrained in the Black psyche, because the stereotypical image, which we have largely internalized, is that Black people are always failing. So we have many individuals who fear success, fear that if you are too successful you will be alienated from Black people. Hence we see individuals failing because the anxiety of possible failure after attempted success is so intense.

What I liked about Muhammad Ali was that he was already free in his mind to speak whatever was on his mind, even if he failed, and even if he said something that was controversial. Malcolm X was the same way. And, to that degree, it freed us up. It was empowering for those of us who wanted to be free from fear and failure.

bh Absolutely. And it was especially empowering to Black men.

CW That was a great contribution, independent of whatever political orientation Ali had, because to oppose the Vietnam War the way he did, and give up three years of his life at the peak of his career, was a tremendous sacrifice born of deep personal integrity!

bh We see this sense of sacrifice expressed in the contributions of a Left activist like Angela Davis. Young folk need to read her autobiography, hear the commitment. A commitment which meant sacrifice, loss, grief, the abdication of privilege.

I think we see this linking of sacrifice, of critical political consciousness with a cultural icon like Martin Luther King. I remember reading and hearing about King during his period of critical reflection on whether or not he should oppose the war in Vietnam, and his recognition that it meant breaking with the conception of a religious leader as politically neutral.

CW That's right.

bh Or more accurately as politically conservative. The choice to oppose the war placed King on the radical edge of progressive politics in the United States.

CW That's so very true. You got that in Fannie Lou Hamer, you got that in Malcolm X, you got that in a Martin Luther King, Jr., a breaking away from fear. In fact, part of the problem, if the truth be told, of Black leadership these days is that they still, in many ways, are confined by certain forms of intellectual and political thought policing that goes on in the Black community.

This happens in relation to the White media as well as the Black community, so that most of our contemporary leaders, by the time they get up to speak, are already in a straightjacket. They already are so tied up in terms of what others are going to think about them, and how it will impose limits on their interests and so forth, that we have no one who, in many ways, is free.

bh This raises again the question of why we must theorize class relations in the Black community. To some extent, what we are really talking about and trying to understand is the way a certain kind of middle-class mentality operates to censor the development of a certain kind of critical oppositional Black intellectuality.

CW The worst feature of the Black middle class is that it refuses to promote self-critical sensibilities, owing to deep-seated anxiety and insecurity over its inability to be fully recognized and accepted by and into mainstream American middle class. We have to tackle this head-on if we are going to break free from the kind of economic/political bondage that has so many of the Black middle-class trapped within the larger capitalist rat race.

bh You embody a challenge to that kind of Black middle-class thinking, certainly as it is enshrined in the academy, in that you candidly position yourself on the Left.

Can you talk about your commitment to Left politics? Where did that come from?

CW Presently, we have Black liberals who remain so preoccupied with race—and race is very important—that the issues of environment, gender, class, and empire tend to be overlooked. We then get those who present themselves as critics, namely, conservatives, who say race is not as important as the liberals think. Instead what is important is individual responsibility. What we have is one set of narrow figures criticized by another set of narrow perspectives.

What the Left presents is a way of fusing personal responsibility and the struggle against racism with a concern for class, gender, and environment, which locates Black people in global debates, but does not lose the global perspective when we talk about the context of our homes, about Black community. Yet this Left vision and analysis is still not available to large numbers of Black people.

bh How do we talk to Black people about what it means to be on the Left? Where does that radical transition take place in our own lives? And to what degree does family background impact on an individual's political orientation?

CW For me, it means picking up where Ella Baker left off, picking up where Martin Luther King, Jr. left off, and picking up where Michael Harrington left off. All three of these individuals were Leftist progressives. All three of these were Democratic Socialists. And to be influenced by these three legacies is to acknowledge the degree to which we have to keep alive a tradition that highlights democracy, which means public accountability especially of multinational corporations; liberty, which means resisting all forms of cultural authoritarianism, be it from the right wing church, Black ideologues, Black nationalists, or mainstream White media. We have to accent liberty and freedom of expression and thought in all of their forms. And I would also suggest that these are three of the richest legacies that have been bequeathed to our generation. Ella Baker, Martin Luther King, Jr., and Michael Harrington.

bh Do you feel that, as Black people, we have a strong tradition in this society of critiquing capitalism, critiquing imperialism?

CW Among our intellectuals, there has been, as we know, a long tradition of critiquing capitalism. In fact, most of our major intellectuals from W.E.B. DuBois to Amiri Baraka to C.L.R. James, have all been part of the socialist tradition. They have not in any way been highly influential in the mainstream of Black America, but they've been exemplary critics of American capitalist civilization. The problem is that any critic of capitalism in the United States is marginalized, and therefore it's very difficult for them to speak a language that is intelligible to large numbers of people. That is the major challenge.

bh Your presence on the Bill Moyers show was really moving because you are on the Left. Watching you I thought, how many times in my lifetime have I been able to witness a Black Left intellectual speaking freely on national TV. How did that interview come about?

CW I think it probably has something to do with the fact that Bill Moyers's assistant Gail Pellet had heard about me and was open to having me on. Bill Moyers himself, being of Baptist origin, felt that I would have interesting things to say, and that I would still be able to speak to the mainstream because of my Christian faith, and because of my relative legitimacy in the eyes of the "mainstream" academy.

bh Certainly you work hard as a member of Democratic Socialists of America, both in a leadership role and in a participatory role. What does U.S. socialism today have to say to underclass Black people? Does it address our concerns as a people?

CW Certainly it does. As an Honorary Chair of Democratic Socialists of America, who talks about the need for redistribution of wealth, resources, and power in this society, I continually advocate public accountability of multinational corporations who have a disproportionate amount of influence on our government as well as our economy, and consequently a disproportionate amount of influence on the quality of life of Black Americans.

These issues speak directly to the plight and predicament of the working poor and Black underclass, because to be poor means to be susceptible to unemployment, toxic dumping, housing shortages, inadequate medical facilities and services, and relatively limited access to resources. So the question becomes where are the resources politically and materially to address these concerns? Most of these resources are found within those corporate centers, and those corporate centers, more and more are emerging, growing, and expanding. So to the degree that these problems plague our communities Democratic Socialists have much to say.

bh What would you say to the young Black person who comes to you either within the academy or coming to hear you give a talk, who says, "I don't know anything about capitalism or socialism as an oppositional response." Where would you send them to develop their critical engagement with Black Left intellectualism?

CW I would have them turn to the Black intellectual tradition of Oliver Cox, the great Black sociologist and his trilogy *Capitalism as a System,* or *Caste, Class and Race*. I would have them read DuBois on *Color and Democracy*. I would have them read your texts and other women intellectuals talking about the intersection of gender, race, and imperialism.

And then I would go on to have them read texts from other traditions that have talked about these same kinds of issues in light of their own heritages, so they get a sense of what the modern world is about. Because the modern world has been primarily about the power of big business, about the expansive possibilities of science and technology. It's also been about the subjugation, subordination, and struggles of working class people, White women, and people of color.

bh But, given the profound and pervasive illiteracy in Black communities, we can't hope to spread a Left message by sending people to books alone. What other alternatives do we have?

CW Yes, I was assuming that this young person was in the process of becoming a literate intellectual, therefore they would be reading. But if you are talking about a brother or sister on the block who may be semi-literate, then we have to talk in terms of mass culture, in terms of popular culture. And here we would talk about music, television, the degree to which we need Black culture workers within the mass media. I cannot emphasize this enough! We must have Black cultural workers within television, film, and video who are presenting alternative perspectives to those who read little—which includes most Americans. We also need more Black journalists who are writing in widely accessible newspapers and magazines.

bh I thought we were going to talk also about the place of film and cinema as a purveyor of knowledge. That we would talk about the need for oppositional Black independent cinema. Let's say we fantasize some kind of Left Black independent cinema, what would that cinema produce? Do we have any examples currently of cinema that politicizes class in such a way that people learn from viewing it?

CW Yeah, I would say that Sankofa's work in Britain would be one example. We don't see it as much as one would like in the Black films made here in the States.

bh We certainly see it in Cuban cinema.

I would include film within the mass media because it plays a very important role. But television is probably the more important in terms of reaching the semi-literate brother and sister on the block.

We are now seeing a kind of flowering of Black cinema, which is wonderful. I think the Hudlin brothers, Camille Billops, Spike Lee, Julie Dash, and others are doing powerful and creative things with Black film.

CW Yet, it is still one part of a larger movement which must take place if we are to talk seriously about radical democratic politics.

bh As I thought about our critical discussion of the Black Left, what kept popping up was our discussion about the resurgence of a kind of Black nationalism that, I think, does speak profoundly and deeply to the Black underclass, and is often heard or read as an expression of, you might say, the height of Black radicalism. So that, when everyday Black people think about Left politics, they usually imagine it expressed in Black nationalism.

Why do you think we are witnessing a resurgence of Black nationalism, and it is politically productive?

CW There are certain myths that we have to dispel. It is not clear that the Black underclass is necessarily inclined towards a Black neo-nationalism. The Black underclass is trying to survive, and much of the Black underclass is linked to all kinds of White power networks through drugs, and what have you, in order to survive. So when one actually looks at what the social bases are for Farrakhan, for example, you'll find that it is predominantly lower middle class. I find the lower middle class to be more inclined towards Black neo-nationalism, because it is they who are most frustrated with trying to gain entree to the mainstream, the White mainstream. And therefore, they are much more anxiety-ridden and much more willing to talk about closing ranks in order to move up within this economic system.

Among young Black people and Black college students today, there is a fascination with Black nationalism of the 60s and 70s. They are inclined to romanticize early nationalism without fully studying the period or the movement. This adds to the current trend towards a superficial neo-nationalism, a nationalism that has more to do with fashionable language and wardrobe, and easy personal catharsis rather than genuine political and intellectual struggle for the redistribution of wealth and power.

As for Black politicians, they are preoccupied with White and Black constituencies and are consequently in compromised positions and therefore they cannot speak with boldness and defiance. They cannot be free in the way I was talking about before. And hence, out of default, Black neo-nationalist spokespersons tend to gain a hearing but not a following. Farrakhan's organization is not that big, but he has many hearers because he speaks with a certain kind of freedom from White control, freedom from White imposition.

bh But I do think we have to remember that he has an audience among Black underclass people because he is on national television so much. And I would like to elaborate on the concept of nationalism because, let's face it, many of the Black underclass, certainly in the South, as opposed to larger northern urban cities, still live in very segregated worlds, worlds where Black separatism is the norm, where people's intimacies, their familiarities are still profoundly rooted by a very race-segregated ethos. So when thinking of Black nationalism, I don't think solely of the expression it takes through the Nation of Islam, but the expression it takes to make Black people define keeping together as a group in order to protect their cultural and material integrity from a hostile White context as important.

CW Right. Black nationalism as a perspective is something distinct from simply Black suspicion of White people.

bh Yes.

CW Preservation of Black cultural integrity, acknowledgement of Black cultural distinctiveness. These two components are important to a broader perspective on Black nationalism. These elements of Black nationalism are indespensable for a progressive Black politics. Yet, a progressive Black politics must go beyond them for purposes of principled coalition and alliance. Unfortunately the dominant forms of Black nationalism tend to be too narrow and sometimes even xenophobic. Yet, this is symptomatic of Black suspicion of White people that is often confirmed by White racist attitudes. And so in that regard, I in no way want to define Black nationalism in terms of these two items.

bh When I reflect critically on the positioning, politically, of a Farrakhan, and the positioning of Malcolm X, it reinforces why we must be ever mindful of history so that people can remember the deep and profound politics of Malcolm X which separate him from a Farrakhan. In fact, what often happens in the world of popular culture and in media representations is that they become transposed in people's minds, making Farrakhan a viable representation of a more contemporary Malcolm X. Clearly, the danger of this takes us back to the importance of literacy. Because only with Black people learning to read the texts of Malcolm X and other Black political theorists can we theoretically advance as a people.

CW In that sense Malcolm and Martin are quite distinct from most of the contemporary Black leaders. Jesse Jackson and Harold Washington are the only ones that comes to mind as able to acknowledge a Democratic Left politics within the context of the Black community, and be consistent about it.

The other thing we have to recognize is that history never repeats itself. There will never be another Malcolm, there will never be another Martin, there will never be another Ella. That it is up to us to forge our own visions and analysis based on the best of what they have bequeathed to us.

This sense of trying to imitate and emulate the past produces a flatness and a banality and becomes at a certain point, simply an empty quest for status, rather than a substantive quest for justice.

bh Cornel, you are outspoken, critical of what you call "a crisis in Black leadership." What defines that crisis?

CW There is a profound crisis in Black leadership, both in terms of quality and vision. We have a leadership that is preoccupied with either being elected to office or sustaining the social base of their organizations. And by that I mean primarily the old line civil rights organizations. There is no one who is willing to be prophetic in a bold and defiant manner with a deep, all-inclusive moral vision and a sophisticated analysis of the distribution of wealth and power and resources in our society. The Black politicians can't do it because they are locked into the mode of compromise; they cannot speak with boldness and defiance, and hence most don't. On the other hand, the civil rights leaders themselves are not talking about class, gender and empire. They don't want to give a critique of multinational corporations, partly because these corporations are helping undergird their own organizations. So they deal with issues of race exclusively, still very important, but also limiting. And of course, there are conservative critics who try to pose as leaders. They talk about issues of self-help. They talk about issues of personal responsibility but they express this in vulgar individualistic terms divorced from collective action and thereby they become darlings of mainstream media for a while.

What we don't have are prophetic voices that are not concerned with being elected to office, that are not concerned with being somehow curtailed by corporate support, but at the same time are deeply moral, deeply ethical, and deeply analytical. Still, I believe there are a whole host of young adults emerging who will provide seeds of hope for the next generation.

bh What do you mean by race-transcending prophets in your essay on the crisis in Black leadership. How is James Baldwin an example?

CW A race-transcending prophet is someone who never forgets about the significance of race but refuses to be confined to race. James Baldwin is in many ways a good example. Why? Because James Baldwin was fundamentally a moralist. And what I mean by that is that he was concerned about the development of each human being regardless of race, creed, gender, and nationality. He felt that racism was a poison that impeded the development of both the racist and the victim of racism.

He never understood Black people solely as victims. But, at the same time, he recognized that part of our plight was to be continually victimized by racism even as we struggled against.

What was crucial was the moral development of the victim and victimizer. So what we need is vision. What we need is getting beyond the confines of race without ever forgetting the impact of racism on Black people in this society.

bh What is the place of humility in the lives of those of us who would be leaders? You say that "to be humble is to be so sure of one's self and one's mission that one can forego calling excessive attention to one's self and status. And even more pointedly, to be humble is to revel in the accomplishment or potential of others, especially those with whom one identifies and to whom one is linked organically. The relative absence of humility in most Black political leaders today is a symptom of the status anxiety and personal insecurity pervasive in Black middle-class America." Can we hope to have more leaders like Malcolm X who don't emerge from Black middle class America?

CW One hopes so. I think we will. But wherever they emerge from, middle class, working class, or underclass—if they are humble, it means they have already reached a certain level of moral maturity. Why? Because humility means two things. One, a capacity for self-criticism. And this is something that we do not have enough of in the Black community, and especially among Black leaders. The second feature is allowing others to shine, affirming others, empowering and enabling others. Those who lack humility are dogmatic and egotistical. And that masks a deep sense of insecurity. They feel the success of others is at the expense of their own fame and glory. If criticism is put forward, they are not able to respond to it. And this produces, of course, an authoritarian sensibility. This is part of our problem in terms of Black leadership, and humility requires maturity. That's why King, Baldwin, and others had reached a level of moral maturity as well as intellectual sophistication.

bh One of the positive dimensions of *Eyes on the Prize* is that we see King the activist walking among the people. No matter how much Black people idealized and idolized him, he did not let that interfere with his perception of himself as a man committed to the struggles of everyday Black people. He never conducted himself as a "famous" leader, he never walked by, or ignored the people he served, he truly felt himself to be one among us.

CW That' s precisely it.

bh He was in collective solidarity.

CW That is precisely right. But you see, there is a deeper issue here when we talk about King in this regard, because King was someone who would enter a church and always dialogue with whomever was there, regardless of what position they occupied. Why? Because King really believed that not only were Black people human, not only did Black people have the capacity to change themselves in society, but that Black people were worthy of the highest forms of love and respect. This is why love was so important to him. Very few Black people and very few Black leaders really believe deeply in the humanity of Black people, believe in the capacity of Black people to achieve and in the love worthiness of Black people. This attitude shows, and Black leaders ought not to think that it doesn't show. King had it, Malcolm had it, Fanny Lou Hamer had it, Garvey had it, Douglass had it. However, not many have it today.

bh You gave almost all male examples. We certainly see that humility in Septima Clark, in *Ready From Within,* where she, as have other Black female leaders in the past, talks about struggling with the conservatism of Black communities that don't think Black women should be engaged in political struggle. And she draws her strength from religious faith; she felt that it was the experience of religiosity that demanded one serve the people, that the true prophet is a servant, and that one must give one's self for the collective good. These notions compelled her to struggle.

One of the things that you say in *Prophetic Fragments* is that your critical acceptance of certain elements of Marxist analysis links you to the world-wide Christian anti-imperialist and anti-capitalist movement, often referred to as liberation theology. I think if we look at liberation theology globally, what is expressed by so many prophets of liberation theology is the tremendous need to maintain one's solidarity with the poor and oppressed, not to stand at a distance, but to place yourself in direct empathy and alliance, by your actions. I think certainly we see this in the work of Gustavo Gutierrez, and we see it in the work of the other liberation theologists.

CW In James Cone, Delores Williams, and others.

bh Certainly when I'm called to talk about the roots of my own critical consciousness, I invariably go back to the Black church, and religion, in general, because it seems to me that the kind of a humility that you speak of comes out of spiritual practice. I often tell people that an exclusively Left approach would not necessarily make me a politically well-rounded and spiritually fulfilled woman. I get that from my experience of religion, of what it means to be a religious person.

How do you perceive the place of spirituality in Black life, in your own sense of religious commitment?

CW First, we have to acknowledge that there is a pervasive impoverishment of the spirit in American society, and especially among Black people. Historically, there have been cultural forces and traditions, like the church, that held cold-heartedness and mean-spiritedness at bay. However, today's impoverishment of the spirit means that this coldness and meanness is becoming more and more pervasive. The church kept these forces at bay by promoting a sense of respect for others, a sense of solidarity, a sense of meaning and value which would usher in the strength to battle against evil.

bh When feminists, particularly White feminists, appropriated the words of Sojourner Truth, they conveniently ignored the fact that her emancipatory politics emerged from her religious faith. People need to remember that the name Isabel Humphrey took, Sojourner Truth, was rooted in her religious faith, that the truth she saw herself seeking was the truth of Oneness with God and her sense that, by choosing God, she was choosing to serve in the emancipation struggle of Black people.

She was also the first Black woman to publicly link the struggle against racism with gender liberation.

CW It's important to talk about these great figures like a Harriet Tubman, Sojourner Truth, or Frederick Douglass, to locate them within a tradition. Because, when we talk about the impoverishment of the spirit of the Black community, we are talking about the waning and eroding of the best of a tradition that transmitted values of struggle, that transmitted ways of life and being to the next generation. And our task is to keep the best of that tradition alive, vibrant.

bh In the past you have talked about "combative spirituality" that seeks to, as you put it, "develop a mode of community that sustains people in their humanity." What do you feel is eroding that kind of dynamic spirituality in Black life?

CW Well, there's no doubt about it, what is eroding it is market forces. What is eroding it is consumerism, hedonism, narcissism, privatism, and careerism of Americans in general, and Black Americans in particular. You cannot have a tradition of resistance and critique along with pervasive hedonism. It means then that we must have spokesmen for genuine love, care, sacrifice, and risk in the face of market forces that highlight buying, selling, and profit making. And poor communities of course have been so thoroughly inundated and saturated with the more pernicious forms of buying and selling, especially drugs and women's bodies and so forth, that these traditions of care and respect have almost completely broken down.

When our grandmothers are not respected, so that mothers are not respected, fathers have no respect, preachers have no respect—no one has respect. Respect is externalized, given to those who exercise the most brutal forms of power. Respect goes to the person with the gun; that's what market forces lead to.

bh If we look at the commodification of religion, that leads us to have the kind of evangelists who, rather than linking religiosity to solidarity with the poor, link it to notions of progress and self-betterment.

CW That's the gospel of wealth and health led by the Fred Prices and others. And unfortunately, we do indeed have very, very strong expressions of gospels of wealth and health which I think have very little to do with the Gospel of Jesus Christ, but that's my own view about it.

bh It's appropriate here to bring up the Gospel of Jesus Christ, because again, when I think of the Christian narratives that formed my own upbringing, when I say to people, you know, I didn't go to thinkers like Gutierrez to learn about liberation theology because I had internalized the chapter in Matthew which said, "Unless you give to the least of these you haven't given to me," in Sunday School.

CW That's right.

bh Which, politically speaking, is a profoundly Left message on communalism.

CW That's true. That's very true.

bh How can Black intellectuals re-awaken concern with that message of communalism and sharing?

CW This is hard, given that the ethic of buying and selling is so pervasive. But don't get me wrong, the younger generation is now moving in very, very, progressive, very, very militant directions. Some of it is misguided, but the spirit of resistance is now emerging in a way that it hasn't in the last 15 or 20 years. This is a salutary development. And it's not just rap music. We have, so-called middle-aged cultural artists like Frankie Beverly and Maze, and Jimmy Jam, Terry Lewis with Janet Jackson's Rhythm Nation album, and we have critiques of Black patriarchy by those geniuses in Atlanta, L.A. Reed and Babyface (Kenneth Edmonds). I mean, all these are forms of cultural resistance that are manifest and that we ought not overlook in the present moment.

bh You have said that you continue to find Christian narratives and stories empowering and enabling. Can you speak about how you feel enabled by those narratives?

CW Well, I feel enabled because I think that when you look squarely and candidly at the human condition, at inevitable death and at the pervasive disease and oppression around the world, that you could quite easily draw an inference that would lead toward pessimism and cynicism, so the question becomes, what are some of the sources that would allow us to fight against and mitigate against the seemingly absurd character of our existence? And I believe that Christian stories and narratives provide insight into our very brief pilgrimage and sojourn on this globe. It provides us with a way to demand that service and sacrifice, care and love sit at the center of what it is to be human. It reaffirms that we are human to the degree to which we love and care and serve. And that is a profound insight. Now I'm not saying that Christianity has a monopoly on this. We also find this in Islam, traditional Yoruba and Fon religion, Judaism, Buddhism, Sufi Mysticism and other religions.

As for me, I've found it in the Christian faith, and I pursue it in light of the Christian faith.

bh This speaks to the meaning of spirituality in contemporary life. We turn to spirituality as an oppositional mode of being that enables us to combat some of the hopelessness confronting us today. You called it "walking nihilism," "the imposing of closure on the human organism, by the organism itself. We are currently in the midst of a lived nihilism. We are talking about real obstacles to the sustaining of a people."

How do those of us who feel we've had that joyous sense of Black community that is affirming, rooted in religious tradition, share that knowledge, that gift, with others?

CW This is one of the reasons why, in some ways, Nietzsche's text on nihilism is so very important, given the lived nihilism in so many Black communities.

I want to suggest that there are only three ways out. All of them are forms of conversion. There is either personal conversion by means of love of another, love of a mother, father, a mate, a spouse, that's strong enough to convince one to shift from a nihilistic mode to a meaningful mode. The second is political conversion, in which an ideology or a cause becomes strong enough to shift from a nihilistic mode to a meaningful mode.

And the third form of conversion is that of religious conversion, be it Christianity or Islam, or any faith that convinces you that there are, in fact, reasons to live and serve, so that one sidesteps the nihilistic traps, be it drugs, alcoholism, or any of the various forms of addiction that are so deeply ingrained in our society. Without some form of conversion, we will simply lose thousands of people, especially Black people. This will have serious repercussions for the next generation.

bh When people talk about the growing popularity of Black women writers, or when they try to contrast that and say somehow Black male writers are receiving less attention, I always find that problematic, because people often don't go on to talk about what it is in these works that are giving them the quality of appeal that we may not see in many works by Black male writers.

And I would say that one of the things that's in all these works is a concern with spiritual well-being. Toni Cade Bambara begins her novel *The Salt Eaters* with the question, "are you sure that you want to be well?" And she is not just talking about physical well-being, she is talking about a well-being of the spirit.

CW That's right. Of the spirit and the soul.

bh Certainly a novel like Paule Marshall's *Praise Song for the Widow* has to do with a politicized spiritual reawakening.

CW I think something else is going on, too. And I think, for example, of Toni Morrison's *Beloved,* in which the love ethic sits at the center. You don't see that kind of self-love affirmed in many works by Black male writers.

bh When I think about *Beloved* I remember that the person who brings the prophetic message of redemptive love, it is the grandmother, in her role of preacher—she goes into the field—and preaches that sermon about the necessity of love.

CW That sermon is one of the great moments in American literature. One of the great moments in modern literature. And you don't find that kind of sermon in a Richard Wright or a James Baldwin or even Ralph Ellison. You just don't find it. There is a depth of love for Black humanity which is both affirmed and enacted that, I think, speaks very deeply to these spiritual issues. And I think this relates precisely to the controversy in the relations between Black men and women.

bh That is exactly what I was going to ask you. What does it mean for a progressive Black male on the Left to ally himself with the critique of patriarchy and sexism, to be supportive of feminist movement?

CW We have to recognize that there cannot be relationships unless there is commitment, unless there is loyalty, unless there is love, patience, persistence. Now, the degree to which these values are eroding is the degree to which there cannot be healthy relationships. And if there are no relationships then there is only the joining of people for the purposes of bodily stimulation.

And if we live in a society in which these very values are eroding, then it's no accident that we are going to see less and less qualitative relations between Black men and women.

At the same time, and this is one reason why I think many Black men and women are at each other's throats, is because there is tremendous rage in Black men.

bh Talk about it.

CW Just as there is a tremendous sense of inadequacy and rage in Black women. That feeling of inadequacy and rage is also in Black men.

bh But this rage takes a different form.

CW That's right. The rage takes a different form, the sense of inadequacy takes a different form.

bh You are one of the few men who's talked about the fact that often suppressed rage takes the form of Black male violence against Black women.

CW That's right, it is one of the most insidious manifestations imaginable. This rage and this inadequacy, when they come up in their raw form in a violent culture means combat. We have always had the rage—don't get me wrong. We have always felt the inadequacy, but we've also had traditions that were able to channel it in such a way that we could remain in that boat with the tension, with the hostility, because there was also love, care, loyalty, and solidarity.

bh Well, one of the things that you talked about earlier and I think you can link that rage to is the whole question of fear and failure.

CW That's right. That's the fundamental problem. This is what Marcus Garvey understood. In many ways he was the first one to understand it. He understood the fact that Black people could only be fully human when they were free enough from the fear and failure which is imposed upon them by a larger racist society, but it would not be a matter of blaming that society, it would be a matter of understanding that society and asserting themselves boldly and defiantly as human beings. Very few Black folk ever reach that level, and more must.

bh I think we also have to break away from the bourgeois tradition of romantic love which isn't necessarily about creating the conditions for what you call critical affirmation. And I think this produces a lot of the tensions between heterosexual Black men and Black women, and between gays. We must think of not just romantic love, but of love in general as being about people mutually meeting each other's needs and giving and receiving critical feedback.

CW That's so, so very true. We actually see some of the best of this in the traditions of contemporary Africa that has a more de-romanticized, or less romanticized, conception of relationship, talking more about partnership. I know this from my loving Ethiopian wife.

bh That's where, as Black people, we have much to learn from looking at global revolutionary struggles, looking at, for example, the work of Nicaraguans. There has to be a re-conceptualization of what it means to be engaged in a primary liberation struggle as we also try to alter issues of gender.

That's what we haven't done enough of yet, theoretically, as African Americans, to begin to conceptualize how we re-envision Black liberation struggle in ways that allow us to look at gender, and the pain that we feel negotiating gender politics.

CW Sexuality in general must be discussed. There is a deep reluctance in the Black community to talk seriously about sexuality. We've got significant numbers of gays and lesbians who oftentimes are rendered invisible, as if their humanity somehow ought to be hidden and concealed.

bh It's interesting when you think about the kind of compassion, love, and openness that many of us remember in the traditional Black church, because in fact we don't remember those Black gay folk as going off to set up a separate sub-culture that alienates and estranges them from Black community. But in fact we remember them vitally engaged in the maintenance and sustaining of Black culture.

CW There's no doubt, good God almighty, if you look at Black music in the Black church and the crucial role that Black gays and lesbians have played there, this is the grand example. And it's the failure of the Black religious leadership to come to terms with these issues of sexuality, but it's also a fear on behalf of the congregation that talking about this may undermine some of the consensus in other areas and thereby render the community less able to confront other issues.

bh So the people won't think I'm stereotyping, when we talk about the roles people play musically, I think that we have to remember that there has always been in the realm of Black cultural production an acceptance of certain forms of radical behavior, behavior that, within the status quo of everyday life, people might object to, but certainly when we look at the tradition of blues singers, the Black women who were cross-dressing, if we look at the career of someone like Josephine Baker, I mean, we see an openness, a tolerance within the sphere of cultural production that may not have made itself known in other spheres of Black life.

CW That is so very true.

bh Well, Cornel, as we bring this discussion to a close, are there any last words that you want to give us? Will we have a renewed Black liberation struggle? Will the struggle take another form? Will it be a more inclusive struggle? Or will we have simultaneous movements?

CW It's hard to say, but, I think the important thing is that we must never give up hope. Black people have always been in a very difficult predicament, we must always preserve our subversive memory, which is to say our attempt to stay in tune with the best of our history. And at the same time we must always be explicitly moral in an all-inclusive manner so that we resist all forms of xenophobia.

bh How do you define xenophobia?

CW Xenophobia is a hatred of the other, be it a hatred of individuals different from one's self, be it a Black, White, Jewish, or Korean person.

All forms of racism must be rejected directly and openly.

I have hope for the next generation. I think that they're up against a lot. Market forces are stronger now than they've been in American history. But I also believe in the ingenuity, in the intelligence, the beauty, the laughter and the love that Black people can give both themselves and to others. And that is the raw stuff out of which any major movement for justice is made.

bh When you talked about the need for a politics that deals with death, dread, despair, disappointment, you talked about the fact that even as we identify strategic conflicts and problems, we also have to identify the location of our joys.

CW That's right.

bh You certainly identified that one way cultural production functions in Black communities is to awaken our joy. And I was thinking, as we close, of the impact of Anita Baker's song "You Bring me Joy."

CW Yes.

bh Which returns us to that notion of redemptive care, reciprocal, mutual, sharing, that brings about a sense of joy. It's the kind of joy and fellowship I feel always in talking with you. Thank you.

CW Thank you.

4

Introduction to bell hooks

She is a friend of my mind.

Toni Morrison
Beloved

The question which one asks oneself begins, at last, to illuminate
the world, and become one's keys to the experience of others.
One can only face in others what one can face in oneself. On this
confrontation depends the measure of our wisdom and
compassion.

James Baldwin
Nobody Knows My Name

bell hooks is a unique figure on the American intellectual
scene. Unlike most academics, she expresses her powerful insights
and provocative arguments in an intelligible prose read by thousands of her literate fellow citizens, yet she is a bonafide member
of the academy—with a Stanford education, a highbrow Ph.D and
appointments at Yale and Oberlin. Unlike that of most men and
women of letters, her accessible language is informed by the best
of recent theory and is inspired by the struggles of everyday African American people. Unlike most Black intellectuals, she writes
with a deep sense of urgency about the existential and psy-
chocultural dimensions of African American life—especially those
spiritual and intimate issues of love, hurt, pain, envy, and desire
usually probed by artists. In short, she brings her enormous re-

sources of intellect, wisdom, concern and care to bear on the quality of life in American society, with a specific focus on that of people of African descent.

This multifaceted uniqueness deserves scrutiny in that it may give some clues to bell hooks's intellectual contributions to our time and the heavy price she pays. First, a few preliminary rules of American intellectual life. In the academy, Black people are usually viewed as guilty (i.e., unable to meet "standards" of excellence) until proven innocent (i.e., taken seriously by the academy). Furthermore, Black women are often perceived as congenitally guilty and hence frequently bereft of serious mentors who believe in their intellectual capacity and potential. These rules are due not simply to the chronic racist and patriarchal sensibilities in the life of the American mind, but also to the instinctive threat Black women's high-quality intellectual presence poses to the interpersonal dynamics of academic culture. The closely-knit communities of intellectuals in American life—which include some Black men—tend to provide little or no space in which Black women's intelligence can be taken seriously, that is, affirmed in a critical mode or contested in an enabling way. At times it seems the mere appearance of linguistic styles and social gestures often characteristic of Black women's cultural life unsettle these academic communities in a bewildering manner.

bell hooks has defied these rules without severing her links to the academy. She has preserved her intellectual integrity alongside her personal rage at these rules which devalue Black women. She has insisted on doing her intellectual work—grappling with questions and issues usually eschewed by the academy—in her own style and in the interests of Black people. It is no accident that certain academics (both White and Black), with their fashionable jargons and hierarchical pecking orders, shy away from her writing, while nonacademic writers and artists devour them. She threatens the prevailing notions of what it means to be an "acceptable" academic and professional intellectual in our time.

This holds especially for Black male intellectuals who are reluctant to view their own social manners and sexual desires as objects of intellectual investigation. The delicate and intimate issues of the anxieties and insecurities that result from coping with the devaluing rules of American intellectual life are often too painful to be examined beyond the bull session or gossip mill. bell hooks courageously brings these ugly silences—the surreptitious self-loathing, the lack of self-confidence which hampers any serious self-probing—to the light of day. She rightly posits that a deliberate Black intellectual blindness toward these matters stunts our growth as thinkers and delimits our contributions to the cause of Black freedom. In short, her regulative ideal is not simply decolonized minds but also decolonized souls and bodies that neither pay homage to White institutions (and their reward structures of prestige and status) nor uncritically celebrate Black culture (with its rampant patriarchal and homophobic practices).

bell hooks's bold project locates her on the margins of the academy and the Black community—in search of a beloved community whose members will come from these very same margins. Her kind of Black feminism—or womanism—puts a premium on reconstructing new communities of Black people (of whatever gender, sexual orientation, and class) and progressives (of whatever race) regulated by thoroughly decolonized visions, analyses and practices. She puts her prodigious readings and prolific writings—already five volumes at her young age—at the service of Black Mundigkeit, i.e., Black maturity, responsibility, and autonomy in the psychic, political, economic, and spiritual spheres.

This project makes tough demands on her, not simply because the two-layered marginality she promotes and lives is difficult, but also because she examines her own lived experiences as occasions from which we may question, probe, and interrogate ourselves. Her poignant and often painful scrutiny of crucial moments in her life is neither self-indulgent nor self-aggrandizing. Rather, these moments are posited as exemplary cultural phenomena that—when analyzed properly—illuminate those unacknowledged realities and hidden injuries that adversely affect us. She probes beneath those smooth discourses and alongside those erudite academic analyses that too often remain uncoded and unread while at the same time profoundly circumscribing these discourses and analyses on conscious and unconscious levels.

hooks is, for example, keenly aware of the degree to which much work in Afro-American studies—especially literary studies—is influence by French theory and German philosophy. She also points out that much of this work was pioneered by talented Black male scholars grappling with the devaluing rules of American intellectual life. Her strategy is neither to prematurely reject these theories and philosophies nor to eschew the efforts of the Black critics—even when this work results in more visibility and prestige than that of her own within the academy. Instead she critically uses these theories and philosophies when and where they illumine, not only in literary studies, but, more pointedly, in film, video, and television studies—areas about which most Afro-American scholars have been silent. She then returns to the work of Black critics to reveal the severe limits of these theories and philosophies when applied to the complexity of Black cultural life. In short, her form of critique neither solely negates nor sophomorically castigates; rather, she creatively appropriates for her purposes. This process not only highlights relentless criticism; it also reinforces enabling forms of critical exchange that expand and empower interlocutors in the dialogue (and readers of her texts).

This is why her books help us not only to decolonize our minds, souls, and bodies; on a deeper level, they touch our lives. It is difficult to read a bell hooks essay or text without enacting some form of self-examination or self-inventory. To look exclusively for argument and evidence in her work is to remain within one dimension of it. As with a Chekhov play or Billie Holiday solo, one must also probe into the complex interplay of circumstance, pain, and resistance. For bell hooks, the unexamined life is not worth living, yet the examined life is full of yearnings, hurts, and hope.

bell hooks is an African American writer without being an Afro-centric thinker; that is, she grounds her interests, concerns and subject matter in Black life yet she refuses to view this life in a competitive relation to European or Euro-American life. Like a jazz musician, she is not afraid of or apologetic for the hybrid character of Black culture. Hence she feels no need to spend her energy fighting off White influences, extricating White elements, or teasing out only African sources for her thought. She is also a Black feminist—or womanist—writer without being a separatist activist; namely, she puts the flowering of Black women's possibility and potentiality at the center of her work yet she refuses to view this flowering apart from the freedom of Black men. Her unflinching stance against patriarchal, class, imperial, and homophobic practices is rooted in a conviction that embraces the Black and progressive communities.

In conclusion, bell hooks's unique contribution to intellectual life, American letters and Black thought is that of producing a challenging corpus of work which proposes a singular human struggle to be candid about one's self and contestatory toward the dehumanizing forces in our world. Her works sing a polyphonic "song of a great composite democratic individual" yearning for a principled connectedness that promotes the distinctive self-development of each and every one of us. And she sings this song in the antiphonal, syncopated, and rhythmic forms bequeathed to her by African foremothers and forefathers who refused to be silent in a strange land of pharaonic treatment. Sing on, bell, sing on!

5

bell hooks Interviewed by Cornel West

CW Begin by telling me what your motivation has been for becoming an intellectual. Talk about your work, and the politics of both your personal relationships and your politics of resistance.

bh A passion for ideas, for thinking critically, lay the groundwork for my commitment to intellectual life. That passion began in childhood. When I was young I had, and continue to have, an insatiable longing to read everything—know everything. To this day I remain the kind of reader for whom nothing is off limits, from children's books, Harlequin romances, car and fashion magazines, self-help books, all kinds of pulp, to economic, sociological, psychological, literary, and feminist theory. I love to read across disciplines. I am always astonished by academics who show no interest in work outside their discipline. For me, reading broadly has been absolutely essential to the kind of speculative critical thinking that informs my work. I have said in other writing that the difficulty many academics have when called to speak and write from an inclusive standpoint—one where ideas are looked at from a multidimensional perspective that begins with an analysis rooted in an understanding of race, gender, and class is due to the gap created by a lack of information. Since so many scholars and academics have been trained to think and study along narrow disciplinary lines, the knowledge they produce rarely addresses the complexity of our experience or our capacity to know. A pure passion to know was the yearning that seduced me into intellectual life. And that yearning has really been the impetus motivating me to synthesize and juxtapose in a complex way ideas, experiences that on the surface might not appear to have a point of convergence.

When I think about my intellectual development, where I am now, I am often amazed that the attitudes and commitments to intellectual work that were present in my childhood remain constant. In Terry Eagleton's essay "The Significance of Theory," he suggests that children make the best theorists because they often possess that unstoppable will to transgress the boundaries of accepted ideas, to explore and discover new ways of thinking and being.

My childhood engagement with ideas was intimately linked to struggle for self-recovery. Growing up in a family with strong elements of dysfunctionality, where I was psychologically wounded and at times physically hurt, the primary force which kept me going, which lifted my spirits was critical engagement with ideas. This engagement and concomitant development of critical consciousness enabled me to step back from the family situation and look at myself, my parents, my siblings from a critical, analytical perspective. This helped me to understand the personal history and experiences informing my parents' behavior. So, Cornel, what has made my relationship to theory unique is the way my life stands as testimony to the positive power of critical thinking.

Coupling a passion for ideas and a vivid imagination, I found in the world of creative writing a place of transcendence, a way to recover myself. Unlike many children in dysfunctional family settings who create imaginary playmates to sustain their spirits, I found early on that intense creative engagement with reading and writing poetry took me on an imaginative journey that uplifted and inspired me. I started writing poetry when I was ten, publishing my first poems in our Sunday school magazine. Receiving such affirmation at such an early age gave me an autonomous sense of self-esteem while instilling in me the understanding that my voice was important, that my vision could be articulated and shared.

I remember growing up in our house on First Street. We had a room for the sick and dying. We called it the middle room. In that room hung curtains with the Elizabeth Barrett Browning sonnet "How do I Love Thee Let Me Count the Ways." I would stand at the window reciting this sonnet over and over again. Reciting poetry was an important cultural practice in both Black schools and homes.

CW Was there a particular person exposing you to poetry at that time?

bh I grew up in the traditional Black church where you learned poems for Easter Sunday, Black History Month, and so on.

The last time I went home to my childhood church, Virginia Street Baptist Church…

CW In Kentucky?

bh Yes. Every Sunday there is a scheduled program when Sunday school ends, where we come up together as a congregation and somebody reports on the Sunday school lesson.

CW Yeah, we did that too.

bh And you might have a play, we used to have plays. And it made me think, who were these adult Black people acting out a play, made me remember that Black adults did these kinds of things as a group, that we had a context to memorize things, that I memorized things.

As an adolescent I went to Crispus Attucks High School, before it was integrated, and we used to have similar programs before pep rallies. In fact, my first memory of major public speaking is during pep rallies. We students would always have a talent show where folks would sing or perform whatever talent they had. My talent, naturally, was reciting poems.

CW Langston Hughes or who?

bh It started out ironically with James Whitecomb Rielly's "The Little Orphan Annie Poem." That was my favorite poem to recite.

CW Really, "Little Orphan Annie?"

bh Yes, because I could act out the parts. And it gave me a little taste of fame in my high school because people knew and liked my recitations.

CW That gave you a certain status.

bh Absolutely. A little notoriety is crucial for adolescent self-esteem. I also read the scripture during the morning offering from the time I was a little girl. I chose the passage from Matthew that goes, "If you haven't given to the least of these my brethren, you haven't given to me."

CW Powerful passage, powerful passage.

bh So here I'd be, a young girl reading scripture while folks would be shouting and the old ladies would be saying, "Oh how she reads!" and this solidified for me the relationship between artistic performance and artistic/intellectual production as forces which deeply move people spiritually and emotionally. This connection really had a tremendous impact on me.

CW Say something about your experience at Stanford and Wisconsin, because it is interesting that, despite this rich grounding in Black civil society, Black family, Black church, Black school, you chose to study at these highly prestigious, predominantly White institutions. How did it affect and alter you?

bh Well, it's very interesting, because I really did not understand class differences among Black people until I went to Stanford. Growing up in segregated Kentucky, it was irrelevant how much money any individual Black person did or did not have because we lived as a community in the same areas and, for the most part, under the same conditions. We all went to the same schools, we attended the same church. So, one could say, my "sense" of Blackness was monolithic, I thought all Black people existed in a kinship structure of larger community. Stanford, was my first real departure from that way of life.

Stanford of the early 1970s had a lot of Black students from the African diaspora. St. Clair Drake was our major scholarly figure, and there were international Black students, as well as wealthy Black American students. It was a very, very difficult time in my life. College initiated my class awakening, shook up my agrarian, working-class notions of privilege, where privilege was defined as enough food, shelter, and care, yet here I was in an institution where "plenty" was defined through vacations in South America and Europe. It is as a result of these vantage points, these experiences, that I came to politically interrogate class differences among Black people. I realized for the first time that Black people, nationally and internationally, are not joined ideologically, politically, or culturally by virtue of skin color but that, in fact, the question of ideology, and political stance would very much determine the degree to which we could be joined together.

Also the years that I was at Stanford, the Black Muslims were a strong force on the campus.

CW Yeah, out in East Palo Alto…

bh Yes. Between Black power, SDS, SNCC, protest against the Vietnam war, and Stonewall, it was a very politicized time.

CW Now, was this class awakening preceded by a feminist awakening or did your feminist awakening develop through a class analysis?

bh My feminist awakening came as a result of growing up in a traditional, patriarchal household. With patriarchy meaning absolute rule by the father. Contrary to most of the studies that have been done by people like Moynihan, Frazier, or people that focus on urban cities, two-parent-headed households were the "norm" throughout my childhood. It is also important to keep in mind that, when we talk about Black people before 1900, at least ninety percent of those Black people were still in the agrarian South and that in Black southern familial tradition, the father was the understood head of the household, whether or not he was an earning provider in the home.

If a sociologist had come into the home of my grandmother or my mother they would have seen strong talking women and very silent men. And they might not have readily understood that any time my grandfather did decide to speak, his word was law. So it was very deceptive if you took that household in terms of how it appeared from an outsider's vantage point. Mother might be doing all the talking, she might also be doing all the apparent decision making. But no matter what my mother had approved of, if my father decided to open his mouth and say no, his word was law. There would be no ensuing discussion or argument about it. So it's really important to keep in mind when we talk about the place of Black males and Black father figures in the home, that many of us are coming from traditional households where the father was not only present but exerting a tremendous amount of authority and control.

CW Are you saying then that there were certain criticisms of Black patriarchy already implicit in your younger years?

bh Now remember, Cornel, I grew up in a household with five sisters and one brother, and we five older girls were seeing this younger brother get to do all kinds of things, get to have all kinds of privileges that we did not have.

We were also witnessing on a daily basis the fierceness of my father. If, for example, my father came home and something was not right about the house he would immediately and sometimes violently upbraid my mother. Instilling in all of us a fear of his moods, his brutal censure.

I can also remember walking up the stairs one day after having a conflict with my mother and saying, "I'm never going to get married, I'm never going to let any man tell me what to do. " I attribute this early consciousness of male domination to my keen sense that inequity in my household was gender based.

Now I would like to add that my maternal grandfather, Daddy Gus, represented an alternative model of Black masculinity. He was always kind, gentle and non-dominating. He really represented for me a non-traditional masculine ideal. Seeing these differing styles of Black maleness has made me ever mindful of the need to resist constructing a negative monolithic paradigm of Black masculinity.

CW How old were you at this time?

bh Sixteen, fifteen, the time when one can begin to feel very acutely the sense of injustice brought about by sex role patterns.

CW With relation to your feminist development, can you share with me what went into your decision to write your dissertation on Toni Morrison?

bh I wrote my first book *Ain't I a Woman: Black Women and Feminism* as a nineteen-year-old undergraduate at Stanford. By then I was heavily engaged in women's studies classes and had begun, not only to think in a more sophisticated way about gender, but also more about the specific nature of Black female reality. This also began the "hot" time, when women of color were telling "women's studies" that they were only looking at White women's experience. Naturally, this brought about the mad search for the authentic Black female voice.

Many people don't think of Toni Morrison as an essayist, but she was really one of the first major Black female voices in social criticism, making specific commentary on gender in the early 1970s and late 1960s. I read her essays before reading her fiction. So, first and foremost, I saw Morrison as a mentor figure, a Black woman writing the kind of social critique I envisioned myself writing.

My favorite novel still is *The Bluest Eye*. Because it does in literature what Black feminists have just begun documenting in the realm of feminist theory, and that is to show graphically the intertwining of race, gender, and class. Early on in the novel there is that powerful moment when Claudia, speaking about her mother, says, "When I think of autumn, I think of someone with hands who does not want me to die." There is that immediate sense of winter, the cold, being poor, and the effect of poverty on the consciousness of young Black girls. I, and I believe many Black women, have an immediate identification with Morrison's novels because she grappled with what it means to be poor and Black, coming to consciousness of a political and sexual world around you.

Despite the clarity and magic in her later works, her first novel *The Bluest Eye* is for me the most powerful. It has a raw, subversive, political immediacy which is not as apparent in her later novels. Although *The Street,* written earlier by Ann Petry, comes close to invoking that immediacy—an opinion I've had the opportunity to share and elaborate on with Ann Petry herself.

CW I remember she came to your class at Yale.

bh It was an unforgettable moment when she stood there and told us that she knew before she had written a word that Lutie was going to kill Boots.

The Street also gives us that powerful intertwining of race, sex, and class. But, it doesn't give us girlhood in quite the same way as Morrison's *The Bluest Eye.* Morrison was trying to delineate, for a country which has historically discarded the experience of Black females, the processes and experiences which construct and shape Black women's identities. She shows fictively ways we make it despite the oppressive conditions of poverty and racial/sexual subordination but she also shows the wounds—the scars we carry into adulthood.

I also came to Morrison believing that White critics, and many of the Black people who were writing about Morrison, were not delving as deeply into the complexity of her work as her writing deserved.

CW But you haven't published any of this work.

bh I have never focused on publishing my literary criticism to the degree that I have feminist theory or cultural criticism, or even film criticism. In fact, I often explain to people that having written books that cut across class barriers makes it very difficult to focus on producing and publishing literary criticism, given its narrow and limited audience.

When *Ain't I a Woman* was first published I would get dozens of letters a week, where, say, a Black woman from a small town, out in the middle of nowhere, would tell me that she read my book at the public library and it transformed her life. Intellectual affirmation of this sort forces you to interrogate radical pedagogy as it relates to your individual notions of intellectual production. I sometimes feel an enormous sense of personal power in a positive way. I feel as though I have enabled some women and men to live more fully in the world. But this has also made it very difficult for me to put one hundred percent of my energy into literary criticism. I continue to write literary criticism but my efforts are directed much more towards that literature which is going to reach a wider audience and serve as a catalyst for personal and communal transformation.

CW With all this debate nowadays about public intellectuals, it is fascinating to see someone like yourself whose texts sell thirty, and forty thousand copies, whose texts sell across the academy and the community, who receives letters from Black prisoners—a brother talking about how your name is a household word in his prison. I can see your point about not wanting to be so narrowly "academicized" that it takes away this much broader audience. There must also be a good deal of tension and anxiety about having such a broad public on the one hand while still negotiating a viable career within the academy. You've written about some of your tensions within the academy, what some of its downfalls are. Can you say more about how you've handled these tensions?

bh I think that the major dilemma is the way professionalization within the academy limits those of us who want to speak to broader audiences.

I think back to the heated debate which centered around my choosing not to use footnotes in *Ain't I a Woman*. I actually spent a great deal of time deliberating on whether or not to use footnotes. I went into various communities and asked non-academic Black people if they read books with footnotes. The majority responded by saying that when they open a book with footnotes they immediately think that book isn't for them, that the book is for an academic person. And I've tried to explain, as well as justify, to, for the most part, academically-oriented individuals that my choice around footnotes was very much a choice informed by questions of class, access, and literacy levels rather than a simple devaluation of footnotes, or "shoddy, careless" scholarship. I am perpetually concerned with what kinds of codes, apart from interest, convey to a group of people the notion that a particular book isn't for them.

Which leads me back to the problem of professionalization in the academy, the editorial practice which would have all our articles sound alike. I was teasing an editor working on a piece of mine to appear in a literary journal about the edit he had done, and I said to him, "You know you've stripped this of my flavor, my essence." And we both laughed because he immediately invoked notions of "standard and rigor," when we both knew what he really meant to say was that my work was too personal, engaging, overtly political, too "Black" to conform to the journal's "style."

After finishing *Black Looks: Race and Representation* I said to myself, the world is going say I'm writing too much. A thought which raised all sorts of questions in my mind about Black women, success, and our sense of entitlement. I wonder if male academics—writers like Noam Chomsky, Fred Jameson, or Edward Said—sit around contemplating whether or not they're writing "too much."

I also live with the fear, like others in the academy, that a heavy-handed professionalism is going to come down on me and tell me that what I've written is of no value. I live with that fear because people who are evaluating you for tenure, for jobs, are not looking at something like the letter from the brother in prison. They're looking at me from the perspective of the journal editor, from the perspective of someone who's likely to say, bell hooks is not academic enough.

These tensions are ever present in a positive and negative way. Not just because I straddle academic and non-academic worlds, but because my voice is also evolving, and I think my new books, *Yearning* and *Black Looks*, are moving, in some ways, in a more "academic" direction. The bottom line is that bell hooks readers who always expect me to be straightforward, who expect me to be less abstract, sometimes have difficulty with these books...

CW How are these two books different from your last three?

bh I am engaging in a much more a traditionally academic discourse to discuss issues of aesthetics. Ideally, what I'm trying to do is bridge these two things, as I say in my essay "Postmodern Blackness," it's not like I'm going to be talking about deconstruction in the academy and then go home to basic working-class Black life and not talk at all about the essay I'm writing on, say, postmodernism. And if folks ask me what postmodernism is, I'm certainly going to find a way to satisfy their curiosity. Yet it is this very transgression of intellectual boundaries that academics often resist most violently. It's not that we as academics are forbidden to transgress, but that the forces of social control within the academy, that would have it be primarily a location for the reinscription of the status quo, place a lot of pressure on people who are trying to speak to many audiences, trying to speak with the kind of poly-vocality and multi-vocality that allow us access to different audiences, to conform or be punished.

Take you, for instance. I tease you about giving up academe and becoming a prophet in the Black community, because I know you have the power to speak beyond Princeton, beyond a White, elitist location. I think that most Black people who enter academe end up being threatened by that access we can have to a world beyond the college or university setting alone.

CW Yes, it's true. Few intellectuals fuse intellectual power with deep moral concern and political engagement. Edward Said is somebody that comes to mind, but for every Edward Said there are one hundred and fifty academicians who, albeit interesting and competent, are narrow. So it follows that for every bell hooks there are one hundred and fifty academics threatened by your "poly-vo-cality."

This brings me to another point. You as a writer have already established a corpus. I won't mention your exact age but it is under forty. This is a very impressive amount of work for someone in their thirties to have achieved, and this corpus does not include your fiction, which remains as yet unpublished. But is the sense many of us share that you have not actually received the kind of critical and intellectual attention your work deserves shared by you as well? I realize I'm putting you on the spot here.

bh Naturally, this raises the questions about the meaning and importance attached to acclaim, recognition, and reward. I believe we are often rewarded in ways that are not visible to a larger audience, but certainly traditional rewards are often withheld from insurgent intellectuals.

Many people think that given the success of my work I must have colleges and universities all over the country anxious to offer me teaching positions, that I must get constant job offers, and an exorbitant salary, yet this is not the case. And often it is on precisely this level that I feel I do not receive enough recognition or material reward for the work that I do. Another example would be the racist process I endured to receive tenure. White academics, some of whom had published very little, demanded proof of my continued intention of writing. Something like the anti-bellum slave auction, when the new master demanded proof of the slave women's fertility. Patricia Williams bears witness to this very process in her insightful and transgressive book *Alchemy of Race and Rights.*

CW Proof? What more "proof" did they need?

bh I think it is dangerous to downplay the significance of recognition and reward, because recognition and reward inspires one to keep going, to keep writing, it confirms that there is a listening audience. So, when one's work is downplayed, or unacknowledged, that has the potential to threaten the artist's sense of agency. As early as 1892, Anna Julia Cooper, in *In a Voice from the South*, was pointing out the fact that Black women are often silenced by the knowledge that there will be no receptive audience for their voices.

When I think about Black people who possess qualities one might define as genius or distinctive creativity, I wonder why many of them don't continue to produce at the rate which their initial promise might suggest. A great deal of it most assuredly has to do with the degree to which they are not recognized, supported (emotionally and materially) and/or encouraged. Understanding this makes me feel very fortunate, even blessed, because when the academy was not recognizing the value and legitimacy of my work, many non-academic folks—Black, White, Asian—were writing to me, telling me how much they valued and appreciated my work, which both surprised and sustained me. It was a tremendous honor because I was very much raised to believe that "a prophet is never received in his own home." I grew up with the idea that it is possible to not be received by the community from which you come. But, happily, my experience has been just the opposite.

There was a point after the publication of my first book, where I felt I couldn't go on anymore because I had been so brutally and harshly critiqued by established feminists. It was really those down-home people who were affirming me. This, more than anything else, brought home for me how important larger reward can be.

When Shahrazad Ali began to appear in *Newsweek* and *Time,* I was very resentful. I thought, here is a woman who's written a book which is completely disenabling to Black people and Black community, and yet she's getting all this play in the press while many Black folks don't even know there is a bell hooks, a Cornel West, a Michele Wallace, a Patricia Hill Collins, a Stuart Hall, a Toni Cade Bambara, an Audre Lorde, and all the Black scholars and thinkers who are working in the interest of renewed Black liberation struggle. It can be disheartening.

CW Precisely. Our influence could be so much greater if, in fact, Black intellectuals had broader visibility in the establishment journals, magazines, etc. Yet I feel it is significant that we do still have many ardent readers without the establishment heralding us in this regard.

And now a quick question about fiction. Very few people know that you write fiction extensively. Who is bell hooks the fiction writer?

bh My fiction is much more experimental and abstract than my social criticism and feminist writing and that has made me much more shy about it.

One of the ideas I speak extensively about wherever I go is the joy of our voices. The fact that we can speak in many different ways. Yet this very asset quickly becomes a liability within a market economy such as this one. Once a corporation or even an independent publishing house can market an author as a specific kind of voice, it becomes a label which is put on you. In fact, it's not very different from Hollywood, where actors constantly struggle to avoid being typecast. Let's face it, it is very hard in this culture for even greatly rewarded writers to write in different kinds of voices. Take someone as distinguished as Toni Morrison: people have come to expect a certain kind of lyrical prose and would be quite shocked and disheartened if Morrison were to alter dramatically the style of her fiction or write nonfiction. Or Alice Walker. The tremendous success of a novel like *The Color Purple* that is very sparse in its language was followed by a very verbose and wordy book like *Temple of My Familiar,* and many people couldn't get through it. So the public developed an expectation of who Alice Walker is, of what her voice is. The fact is, most of us Black folks who are coming from working-class and poor backgrounds speak in many voices; we have Black vernacular speech as well as a more standardized speech we can use. What we want is to have the capacity to use all those voices in much the same way as great jazz musicians like pianist Cecil Taylor do in their music.

I read an interview with him in *Downbeat* where he talks about playing White Western classical music as well as a whole range of other things. The joy of his life as a musician has been that capacity to exercise his range. Sadly enough, we haven't gotten to a place in U.S. society yet where we allow Black writers of any status and fame to write in the many voices which they may want to and/or are capable of writing in.

CW Will you publish your fiction under bell hooks? Why don't you publish under your real name, Gloria Watkins?

bh Right now I publish everything under bell hooks, but I would like to publish under even another name. I like play.

CW Tell me again why you chose the name bell hooks over the name given to you by your mother and father?

bh Growing up, I was a sharp-tongued kid. (Some people still think I'm a sharp-tongued woman.)

bell hooks, who I don't remember clearly, was my great grandmother. She was still alive when I was a tiny girl and I remember going to the corner store one day and as usual talking back to my mother, and the storekeeper immediately said, you must be bell hooks's granddaughter, he recognized that sharp tongue.

bell hooks really entered my mind as that figure in my childhood who had paved the way for me to speak. I am, in the African tradition, in the African American religious tradition, very conscious of ancestor acknowledgment as crucial to our well-being as a people. When I think back to the past, to my father's mother Sister Ray, Bell Hooks my great-grandmother, and Sarah Oldham my mother's mother, I think about women who have charted the way for me. Alice Walker, in her essay "In Search of Our Mother's Gardens," articulates that Black women come from a legacy of women who have made a path for us. Take the title of Beverly Guysheftall's early edited anthology, *Sturdy Black Bridges*, where she is saying our mothers have been bridges that we walked across. The world never heard of Bell Blair Hooks and yet it was this woman of fiery speech who transmitted to her daughter Sarah, and her daughter Rosa the capacity of strong speech. These women are the ancestors who make it possible for me to be who I am today.

As a girl we were required to enter my grandmother's house in the African way, so that if we had brought a little friend with us we had to first present them to my grandmother, who would inevitably ask, "Well who are her people?" And then our friend would have to go down the line of her relations. If you walked into the house and you did not acknowledge the elders first, you were punished. I would often think about this later when I went into feminist classrooms where we would do an exercise to test our knowledge of our mother's ancestral lines. Frequently, women didn't even know the name of their great grandmother. It is out of that spirit that I chose the name bell hooks.

The thing I like about the interviews with myself at the end of *Yearning* is that I try to convey my more playful side. I use Play here with a capital P. I think that there is an element of Play that is almost ritualistic in Black folk life. It serves to mediate the tensions, stress, and pain of constant exploitation and oppression. Play, in a sense, becomes a balm; in religious terms, we say there is a Balm in Gilead.

Black folks release the stress and tensions in their lives through constructive Play, and I 've tried to keep that element alive in my life.

Yet, this also raises again the question of what does it mean for us as Black people to function in predominantly White institutions when one of the elements of Black consciousness that is very threatening to a White supremacist world is that spirit of Play? And it is threatening precisely because that spirit of Play is enabling, it enables you to lift yourself up when things seem down, to laugh, to perhaps joke about something which is very serious.

We have talked a great deal about nihilism as it is happening in Black communities, yet one of the forces that nihilism threatens to check is our capacity to Play. If we look at new books like Bernie Siegel's *Love Medicine* and new books on health, we see White psychologists and self-help gurus acknowledging the degree to which thinking positively enables one to survive, the degree to which positive approaches to illness and suffering enable one to transcend and heal. What is so threatening about the nihilism in Black life is that it intervenes on our capacity to think positively, create interludes of Play.

When I was young my brother would tell stories, or act out a play and lift our spirits up, lift us out of the doldrums. Now television and mass media have intervened, robbing us of the ability to share and interact to create enjoyment for ourselves.

I teach a seminar on Zora Neale Hurston, and my students always become annoyed because I try to show them how Arsenio Hall and Eddie Murphy's popularity is rooted in their use of these very kinds of traditional Black "signifying" and Play. Frequently, they take a serious subject and find an element in it that allows one to laugh, lifts one up. And I appreciate that about Arsenio, although his politics are often retrograde.

A scene in that righteously bad movie, *Harlem Nights*, really captures what I'm saying. Arsenio is in the cab weeping over the death of his male buddy, and his grief is rendered comic. The comedy lifts you up, breaks through an otherwise tedious film. It was a particularly Black form of dealing with the absurdity of our lives at times.

What has also handicapped us historically is that elements of Play have not been a part of the White supremacist Euro-centric mode of discourse within the academy. So, to some extent, social mobility required us to enter into a social contract where we suppress both the capacity and the desire to engage in cultural rituals of Play. Signifying is a skill, a method of disengagement which allows you to unwind. I think of it as breakdancing, an art where you see the body deconstructing itself, so to speak, showing you how you can move and control parts of a body one didn't realize existed within the realm of self-discipline or control.

CW Yes, you have a wonderful fusion of transgression, on the one hand, but also a way to hold the demons of meaninglessness at bay, on the other hand, which you are calling the absurd.

Looking at Spike Lee, it has always struck me that Spike's great talent, almost near genius, is his keen sense of Play and the comic. Unfortunately this is fused with retrograde sexual politics and a limiting, neo-nationalist orientation.

bh I would agree, Cornel, Spike is a genius when it comes to documenting that element of Play.

CW And that is one of the main reasons I still go to his movies. This issue of Play is crucial to discussions of Black cultural identity and survival. I'm very glad you brought it up.

Let's return to your work. The degree to which you infuse a kind of spirituality, through the integration of existential issues, issues of psychic survival, the absurd, political engagement, and a deep sense of history. Those levels are interwoven in so many ingenious ways in your work. Take for instance the devaluation of Black women which has been overlooked by White establishment but which has also been overlooked by male-dominated Black nationalist politics. How can we as a people talk seriously about spirituality and political engagement in order to project a future, while simultaneously coming to terms with the past?

bh It's interesting to me that you should combine discussion of Black spirituality with the devaluation of Black women because one of the things I've tried to say throughout my work, when I've talked about religion is that however we might fault the Black church, it has always been a place where Black women have had dignity and respect. Growing up with a sense of the value of Black womanhood came, in part, from the place I saw Black women hold in the church. I think it is very hard for many people to understand that, despite the sexism of the Black church, it was also a place where many Black women found they could drop the mask that was worn all day in Miss Anne's house; they could drop that need to serve others. Church was a place you could be and say, "Father I stretch my hands to thee," and you could let go. In a sense you could drop the layers of daily existence and get to the core of yourself.

The degradation Black women may have experienced in daily life would fall away in the church. It was noting this difference as a young woman that made me think about how the larger society devalues Black womanhood—a devaluation that is perpetuated in our own communities.

What gives me some measure of hope is seeing Shahrazad Ali on the Phil Donahue show with Haki Madhubuti and hearing him say that he did not sell *The Black Man's Guide to Understanding the Black Woman* in his bookstore because it advocated violence against Black women. A subversive and important moment which was undercut when Donahue rushed in and said, "That's censorship." It's telling that a White male "liberal" can make the issue of censorship more important than violence against Black women. We are still in a society were violence against Black womanhood is seen as unimportant, not worthy of concern. Pearl Cleage's short book of essays, *Mad at Miles*, addresses the way violence against Black women is often not taken seriously in our communities—particularly by men.

What I wanted so much to do in my first book was to say there is a history that has produced this circumstance of devaluation. It is not something inherent in Black women that we don't feel good about ourselves, that we are self-hating. Rather it is an experience which is socially circumscribed, brought into being by historical mechanisms. I have to acknowledge here, Cornel, that writing *Ain't I a Woman* was an expression of spiritual devotion to Black womanhood.

CW Would you say your political identity was nascent then?

bh Yes, I was reading Browning and Yeats, very much like Baraka when he was shaping his writerly sensibility. I was reading Wordsworth and Dickinson, I even had this sense that the writer could be removed, "objective." When I began confronting the reality of living as a Black woman in a White supremacist, capitalist patriarchy, the notion of "objectivity" vanished. I wrote *Ain't I a Woman* because I felt called to illuminate something that would change how people perceived Black women. The passage in the Bible that spoke to me during this period was Jacob wrestling with the angel. When the inner call to write that book came to me it was very much like an angel I had to wrestle with.

One of the most important books in my transformation as a young woman in college was *The Autobiography of Malcolm X*. Part of why I wrote the essay "Sitting at the Feet of the Messenger" is because people forget that as Malcolm was coming into his critical consciousness around the issues of capitalism and White supremacy, he was also grappling with himself as a spiritual human being and his sense of spiritual quest. So it makes sense that he was a powerful mentor for me because he grappled with history and his personal place in history.

The kind of organic intellectuality that you so often speak about we see personified in Malcolm's commitment to self-education while in prison. It was also an occasion for him to rethink his relationship to religiosity and spirituality. People don't talk about those passages where Malcolm tells us he could not get down on his knees and pray in the beginning, and the process of conversion and myatonia that came into his life, enabling him to participate in the experience of humility.

CW This is what strikes me as being unique about your work, that in your four volumes critiquing European imperialism, critiquing patriarchy, critiquing class exploitation, critiquing misogyny, critiquing homophobia, what I discern, as well, is a preoccupation with the dynamics of spiritual and personal change so that there is a politics of conversion shot through the political, economic, and social critiques.

When you talk about Malcolm in this way (hardly anybody talks about Malcolm in this way), it makes me think how so many of our dynamic young folk who have been politicized in the last few years by the Chuck Ds, Public Enemies, and others have missed that dimension of Malcolm, have disregarded or misunderstood his politics of conversion. As African Americans, we have yet to talk enough about how individuals actually change, the conversion of the soul that must occur before the role of love and care and intimacy can be meaningfully talked about.

bh I would start with the question of devotion and discipline because when I look at the evolution of my identity as a writer I see it intimately tied to my spiritual evolution. If we think of the slaves as bringing to new world Christianity a sense of personal relationship with God, evidenced most easily in Black spirituals like the one that says, "When I die tomorrow I will say to the Lord, Oh Lord you been my friend." This sense of immediate connection, we find again when we look at mystical religious experience globally—Sufism, Islamic mysticism. The idea that it is not our collective relationship to God that brings about enlightenment and transformation, rather our personal relationship to God. This is intimately linked to the discipline of being a writer. Which is also why it is important to understand the role of solitude and contemplation in Malcolm's life.

One of the things that is very different in my life from the life of my siblings is this ability to be alone, to be with my inner self. When we talk about becoming an intellectual, in the real life-enhancing sense of that word, we're really talking about what it is to sit with one's ideas, where one's mind becomes a workplace, where one really takes enormous amounts of time to contemplate and critically reflect on things. That experience of aloneness undergirds my intellectual practice and it is rooted in spiritual discipline where I have sought aloneness with God and listened to the inner voice of God as it speaks to me in the stillness of my life. I think a great deal about young Black folks engaged in intellectual/artistic production, and wonder if they understand the story of Christ going into the desert, if they know an inner place of absence in which they can be renewed and experience spiritual enlightenment.

CW How do you reconcile those crucial points about solitude with community and the emphasis Black people have on community?

bh I've certainly engaged fully with a number of religious traditions, but in all of them one holds up the notion that when you are truly able to be alone in that sense of Christ going into the garden of Gethsemane or going into the desert, or Buddha sitting under the Boti tree, it actually enables you to re-enter community more fully. This is something that I grapple with a great deal, the sense of collective communal experience. The great gift of enlightenment for whomever it comes to is the sense that only after we are able to experience ourselves within a context of autonomy, aloneness, independence, are we able to come into community with knowledge of our place, and feeling that what we have to give is for the good of the whole. Think, for example, of the question of what it means to save someone's life, which was raised in *Mo' Better Blues*. In order to intervene and save someone's life, one must know, first of all, how to take individual accountability for who we are, for life choices we make. I see how questions of accountability affect my own relationship to community precisely because as I develop intellectually and spiritually, I need greater periods of time alone. And it seems the greater my need to be alone, the greater my need to re-enter community as well.

CW Yes, this is the paradox of writing.

I wanted to say a word about your breaking the silence, as it were, around homophobia in the Black community. And by breaking the silence I don't mean to imply that homophobia hasn't been talked about because there are a number of published works by Black gays and lesbians. Rather, I mean breaking the silence as a heterosexual intellectual who takes the issues of sexual marginalization and devaluation seriously.

What went into your political decision to break this silence?

bh I'd like to give some background on this. Like so many Black folks from traditional communities, I grew up knowing that, say, the schoolteacher across the street was gay and being taught to respect him.

One of the things that hurt me most when *Ain't I a Woman* was first published without any specific commentary on lesbianism was that many Black lesbians such as Barbara Smith and Cheryl Clark actively decided to label me homophobic. That was particularly hurtful because I had lived my life in solidarity with gay and lesbian Black folks. Yet, I was not silenced by their critique; instead I was challenged to ask myself whether or not it is enough to engage in acts of solidarity with gay people in daily life if one does not speak publicly in such a manner that it mirrors those acts of solidarity. This led me to feel that it is important for me to speak openly and publicly about solidarity with gay people, and solidarity around the question of radical sexualities in general. Take for example brother Harlem Dalton's piece, *AIDS in Blackface,* which is one of the pieces in which we're seeing more of us speak openly, not just giving lip service to homophobia, in order to analyze what is making the Black community so homophobic. What is making popular, young Black culture so homophobic? Why are gays such a target for young rappers and Black comedy today? We've got to study these questions in a deeper manner so that we can come to grips with the question of homosexuality in Black community as something that has always been an aspect of our life. I actually feel that, as we have been more integrated into White society, we have actually adopted certain constructs of homophobia that were, in fact, inimical to early forms of Black cultural life. Toni Morrison, certainly, in editing the *Black Book* has spoken to this. Certain forms of persecution of the "other" in traditional Black life based on differences were held in question. There was a real sense of solidarity with anyone who was disenfranchised. I really see us altering that perspective as we enter a middle-class location and sensibility.

CW When you think, for example, of Black institutions, family, and church they are primarily patriarchal. This means there had to be a notion of the "other" and a subjugation of that "other" in order to maintain power.

bh But you never think about the fact that until racial integration every gay Black person in America lived within those families, those institutions, and what I'm saying is that while there was not public acceptance, there was integration into the life of the community. No one got up on Sunday mornings to beat up the Black gay piano player, or call him out.

CW That's true, but let's not glorify that past either, there were sermons preached against homosexuality, and the gay church organist or the lesbian singer could not live an "out" life. It was an understood contract: if you kept it to yourself and sat there quietly listening to the preacher haranguing homosexuality, you were allowed to participate fully in community life. There was integration and respect for gay and lesbian humanity, not lifestyle, and the price for that community acceptance was silence.

bh We have to distinguish between respect for an individual's humanity and respect for an individual's sexual preference. Yet, what I am trying to suggest is that now there is not even respect for gay humanity.

A very poignant essay in Spike's *Spin* issue focusing on gays and AIDS told the story of a Black man who was ostracized and shunned by Black community, and how painful and devastating that was. We need to call upon a traditional Black value system that did, in fact, maintain that no matter what is ailing you (and here we're talking about disease and traditional responses to diseases such as tuberculosis and leprosy), you were still a member of the community and therefore entitled to both care and dignity. There was a magnitude and a generosity within Christian love that could make one reach out and care for people around one. What we are seeing today is a complete breakdown of an ethics of care and responsibility. Today in Black communities we are seeing an ethic imbued with notions of "persecute the outsider," "persecute the different," some of which has to be the outcome of racial integration, where we have, in effect, come to condone and accept levels of persecution in our own daily life that at other historical moments would have been unthinkable.

CW I agree.

bh For instance, why is it that, when a Black person in a predominantly White institution sits at a cocktail party and hears derogatory statements made about Black people, they don't jump up and fight? And yet, forty years ago, it would have been unthinkable for a White person to say, in the presence of Black people, some of the same things which are said to us today. Take, for example, Madonna's *Truth or Dare*. This means, that, to some extent, we have, in consumer society, been made to feel that if we are being paid, we should be willing to submit to certain forms of degradation in exchange for that pay. This economic co-optation desensitizes us and diminishes our feelings of bondedness with all people who are oppressed and abused. It makes us more willing to persecute those that are oppressed and abused because we are ourselves submitting to certain forms of abuse on a daily basis.

CW Again, I agree, but I would like to come back to the issue of sexuality because talking about homophobia in the Black community actually raised the deeper issue of sexuality in general, and why it is that for Black Americans historically there has been the refusal, inability and/or fear to engage in shared public reflection on sexuality. Is this so because, in dealing with sexuality, there is a perceived threat to a certain kind of narrow conception of community that has traditionally held Black people together?

bh One of the things we are in great need of is a discourse that deals with the representation of Black bodies. It is no accident that one of the major themes in Shahrazad Ali's book is the body. By calling into question the way we confront our Black female bodies, Ali takes us back to those 19th century themes of White supremacy: the iconography of Black bodies as represented in the White supremacist imagination. We are doomed to silence and certain forms of sexual repression until we as a people can speak more openly about our own bodies and our notions of the body in general.

It has been painful for me to hear Black women say, for example, "Well there is some truth to what Shahrazad Ali says." In order to respond and intervene I find that I must enter into Ali's discourse directly and take on, say, the issue of Black women and body odor. I respond by saying that while we know fear and stress produce ceratin kinds of body odor it would be quite a different thing if Shahrazad Ali were problematizing the question of body odor in her critique. Perhaps saying instead that many Black women may have a distinctive body odor because we live in a society where we are continually and perpetually under a great deal of stress. Under a great deal of stress, in fact, about negative, White supremacist representations of our bodies.

What Black scholar has done any meaningful anthropological work around obsessive cleanliness in Black Life?

I was visiting a Black woman friend of mine last weekend and we were laughing about how Black people always say, "Don't sit your butt on my bed." We can't fully understand why we find it difficult to publicly discuss sexuality if we don't look at some of our relations to the body and to disease. What do we think is going to happen if someone "sits their butt on your bed?"

CW Do you think this raises the question of sexual taboo?

bh The pervasiveness of AIDS in our community is really requiring that we have some open discussion of how we have sex, who we have sex with, and what sexuality means in our lives.

What does it say about Black male sexuality when many Black men feel desexualized if called upon to use a condom? What kinds of sexuality are we speaking about when Black men feel intimidated sexually by any form of birth control? We can see these notions of sexuality as almost archaic in Western Culture today, as it is imperative for our health that we seek to understand the origin of these beliefs.

One of the major ironies of groups like 2 Live Crew is the representation of an openness about the body and of sexual graphicness which belies the reality of Black life. We know that even basic nudity is still seen by many Black people as an affront and assault on their sensibilities. In most Black homes, across class, there is tremendous unease in relation to the body, nakedness, and the representation of Blackness.

CW Part of this comes from White supremacist discourse associating Black being with Black bodies, as if we have no minds, no intelligence, are only the sum total of our visible physicality, and therefore the issue of whether Black people actually like and love their bodies becomes a crucial thing. I'm thinking specifically about the sermon that you invoked earlier in *Beloved*.

bh Oh, absolutely, which is all about the body.

CW Which is all about the body, and this is fascinating because Toni Morrison would say, "Look you've got to love yourself not only in the abstract; you've got to love your big lips; you've got to love your flat nose; you've got to love your skin, hands, all the way down." The issue of self-regard, self-esteem, and self-respect is reflected in bodily form.

bh This is interesting, because, when I teach *Passing*, Nella Larson's novella, in my introduction to African American literature class, I find that students are very resistant when I ask them to think about the fact that Clair, who has passed for a White ruling-class woman, but who comes back to Blackness, is the only character to really say, "I want to be Black so much I'm willing to sacrifice my husband, my child, my wealth, to live in Harlem." I ask them to think about whether or not she falls to her death because in a White supremacist country, the Black person who is most threatening is the one who loves Blackness, who loves the embodiment of Blackness, the mark of Blackness on the skin, in the body. Cornel, my students could not deal with that. It was as though I were speaking taboo.

Do we fundamentally live in a culture where a Black person who deeply and profoundly loves Blackness is completely at odds with the culture on the whole? Is there no place for Black self-love in this culture? We are in a strange historical moment, in that Blackness is so openly commodified and simultaneously despised. Which should lead us to ask ourselves whether or not it is commodified in a manner that allows us to celebrate Black self-love, or does commodification once again reduce Blackness to spectacle and carnival? Which makes the commodification by White or Black culture not a gesture of love, but really a gesture of disdain.

I believe we are currently engaging a reinscription of the minstrel, particularly B-boy culture, where certain forms of bard suggest a celebration of Blackness. Yet once they are commodified and sold to us in certain forms, do they still carry a message of "Black is so fine, it's so wonderful to be Black?"—or do they carry that sense of spectacle where one might want to engage Blackness as a moment of transgressive pleasure without wanting to truly incorporate Blackness into one's life?

CW This is a crucial issue, which has to do with how we relate to a traditional Garvey, and Malcolm X, and Elijah Muhammad, other Black radicals who, despite their flaws and foibles, had a profound love for Black people and Blackness itself. Which is also why they are currently being appropriated in a gesture of fashion politic and flattened out into objects that no longer represent that uncompromised love of Blackness.

This also leads us to the issue of Black male/female relations. We've heard so much today about the crisis of the Black man and the Black woman, about the nihilism which is so much at the core of today's Black relationships. Could you tie together questions of Black self-regard and Black self-respect as they pertain to Black men and women forming and sustaining loving relationships?

bh In *Sisters of the Yam: Black Women and Self-Recovery* (a manuscript only recently completed), I talk extensively about how Black women's self-recovery informs to a large degree their ability to choose psychologically healthy partners and sustain relationships with them. I believe that it is impossible for two individuals not committed to their own and each other's well being to sustain a healthy and enduring relationship. I am also working on a book which I'm tentatively calling *Black Revolutionary Consciousness,* where I assert that mental health is a crucial frontier in new Black liberation struggle. The key to the sense of what it means to be critically affirming of Blackness; loving of Blackness lies in enhanced psychological health.

One of the things that really profoundly disturbed me was hearing a White woman scholar, Barbara Bowen, give a talk on 16th century misogynist pamphlets written as tracts to define women's place. She read one about tongues, how, if a woman talked too much, she was seen as less chaste and less worthy, and realizing just how historically linked this was to Shahrazad Ali's book, in that both represent misogynist tracts from different historical periods.

I was also fascinated by how Ali's book is represented to us as though it is opposed to a Euro-centric perspective when, in fact, it is completely rooted in a Euro-centric notion of the body. There is so little difference between these 16th century renaissance tracts about the female body and Ali's work. It allows you to realize that, without psychoanalytic exploration of the body, there can be no liberating discussion of gender relations in the Black community.

In *Black Looks,* I write an essay on Black men, and in it I say that what I found particularly moving in *Harlem Nights* was the way in which Quick, played by Eddie Murphy, only divulges his real name to the Black woman that he desires. And in that moment we see cinematically represented the dropping of the mask of masculinity and we see loving recognition. She goes on to repeat his name and he tells her it sounds wonderful when she says it. I chose to interpret that moment as saying to Black people that in the act of recognizing one another, we can also accept ourselves fully. Yet this liberatory message is undermined because her character goes on to betray him. Leaving us with a bleak vision of Black heterosexuality that tells us, when we drop the mask of our false selves in order to display our authentic selves, our authentic sense of being, we will be betrayed, we will be abandoned.

We really have got to begin to look at those psychoanalytic notions of how the self comes into being through a world of recognition and response, through being seen and loved as you really are. We are so obsessed as Black folks with appearances, with surfaces, so where then does that deep and profound inner recognition come from? We see this emotional dissonance in Black parenting, adults obsessively dressing Black children in fashion outfits. These are the ways in which we convey to kids early on that it is the surface representation of yourself that matters most, while the inner self is often left wanting, left without a sense of secure identity. Much of my new work is trying to look at this.

Mo' Better Blues is fundamentally a depressing film because the film ends with a sense that all we can reproduce is that which in the past has already wounded us. There is not a sense that we can revision the past.

Morrison has also pushed us to remember the past in ways and reinterpret it in ways that enable us to seek our own psychic healing.

One of my favorite albums is *Sexual Healing* by Marvin Gaye. For him also there seemed to be the sense that there is a sickness of the body, sickness within the body that affects the body politics. There is a way we can read "Sexual Healing" as not just being about literal desire, sex. Rather, Marvin Gaye was trying to communicate to Black people that there is a sickness in our body politics. The body politic of Blackness is in need of healing and he connects that to a notion of Christ as giving us the capacity to rejoice, similar to Baby Sugg's sermon in *Beloved,* saying we must be grateful for the bodies that we inhabit.

CW That's true, and yet I think the other side of Marvin's attempt to fuse spirituality and sexuality, the negative side, is that sexuality becomes an escape from a confrontation with the disease of the soul. The body then becomes a displacement from a grappling with that nihilism and hopelessness, making sexuality the only means by which one feels one can remain alive, given the living deadness of one's own being.

bh That is the critical tension; that's exactly what we are talking about. In my essay on Black men, I say it is no accident that young Black men have come to represent the outer limits of transgression, ie., *Nasty As You Wanna Be, In Living Color,* etc. The young Black male body becomes the quintessential sign of moving beyond all limits. Perhaps this has been inscribed today because young Black men are threatened daily by violent death and disease.

In Elaine Scarry's book *The Body in Pain* she says that this culture doesn't have a language to articulate pain. An interesting point if you then apply it to the public representation of the young Black male body, through rapping, dancing, sports, a body that has a joy in living yet the daily circumstances of Black male life in the United States is not joy but the constant threat and seduction of death. And this is the tension we see in a figure like Marvin Gaye, who has a range of issues, including substance abuse, yet still identifies the crucial spiritual/sexual question for healing as coming to terms with the body. Which, of course, we know he failed to do within his lifetime.

CW Yes, another Black genius, robbed of his ability to live out, in your words, "the promise of that genius."

One question about your own life. I think continually, incessantly, and obsessively about the title of James Baldwin's book *The Price of the Ticket*. One of the fundamental things about Black intellectual life is the cost that one has to pay for prophetic vocation, and we know James Baldwin himself paid a very high cost for that. How would you begin to talk about the price of the ticket, the price one has to pay as a prophetic intellectual?

bh Well, I already answered that when I spoke earlier about discipline, solitude, and community. The Buddhist monk Thich Nhat Hanh says that when a person decides to truly be themselves, they are going to find themselves alone. I think often about Martin Luther King's decision to oppose the Vietnam War and how his speeches were tied to a certain sense of isolation. He says in his sermon that many preachers will not agree with him and he will find himself alone, at which point he quotes that famous passage from Romans, "Do not be conformed to this world but be ye transformed that you may know what the will of God is, that which is good and perfect…" I have grappled with an enormous sense of isolation. We've had many Black women academics but, to some extent, we are a new generation. We represent the first generation of Black women thinkers who don't have to have children, or manage a household, if we choose. Molly Haskell, a White woman film critic, says, "To claim one's strength as a woman is a fearful thing. Easier to idealize the man or denigrate him, worship at the feet of male authority than explore and exhibit one's own soul, luxuriate in one's own power and risk ending up alone. Once we take responsibility for our mental processes we take responsibility for our lives, that is what is feminism has become for me, looking fiercely and accurately not passively and defensively at the pattern of our lives and acknowledging all the ways which we are not victims but are responsible for the way which we connect the past to the present." These words moved me deeply because I think one of the costs that we pay for uncompromised intellectual pursuit is certain forms of isolation, where, if one does not take care to find community, can be very disenabling and debilitating.

CW Which community does one re-enter with this kind of critical consciousness, this kind of prophetic vocation?

bh Part of the joy of having these kinds of conversations with you is that this is a form of re-entering community. One of the things I sometimes say teasingly to myself is, I take my community where I find it. I used to have very utopian, idealized notion of community, long for the perfect relationship—me and another bohemian Black male intellectual, within the perfect Black community of like-minded souls. Now I'm learning to be nourished from wherever that sense of community comes from, and this way of thinking has enlarged my community. For too long we have conceptualized the Black community in narrow terms. We conceptualized it as a neighborhood that is all Black, something as superficial as that. When, in fact, it seems to me that it is by extending my sense of community that I am able to find nourishment, that I am able to think of this time spent with you in conversation as a kind of communion.

I think back to why we considered calling our dialogues together *Breaking Bread*—the sense of taking one's nourishment in that space where you find it.

6

Dialogue Between bell hooks
and Cornel West

In a society increasingly populated by peoples of color, by those who have known the disdain and domination of the Euro-American world, it would be fascinating to ponder self-love as a religious calling. How are people, beginning in their earliest years, nurtured to act with self-respect and self-responsibility? How are they encouraged to move through the world with a spirit which un-self-righteously challenges everything that threatens to crush the human spirit, the human ability to love ourselves and others? Can we explore such fundamental questions with our students, wondering aloud with them about the fascinating possible spiritual connections between the capacity to love ourselves and the willingness to love and serve others?

Vincent Harding
Hope and History

bh Do you think this resurgence of narrow Black nationalism is in part a response to the feeling many Black people have that we've lost a true sense of community? Are we reaching to national-ism to regain some sense of kinship and bonding?

CW On the one hand, it's a positive move to once again place serious political reflection and action center stage. On the other hand, you are absolutely right, Black neo-nationalism is very narrow and tends to want to recover historical icons without seriously recovering the historical context in which these icons emerged. But most importantly, it is symptomatic of a need for community and all of its meanings: primordial bonding, support, sustenance, projection of a future and, of course, preservation of hope. You see this desire manifested in Spike Lee's nationalism, and you hear it in the lyrics of various rappers across the country.

bh Let's discuss in greater depth the issue of *Spin,* guest edited by Spike Lee, because we both had a similar response to it. Like his films, I was impressed simply by the array of Blackness. Spike consistently provides that space where we can see and acknowledge fully our beauty, the glory of our collective presence. *Mo' Better* was a panorama of Black elegance and that sight alone is aesthetically uplifting.

CW I agree.

bh And yet what made the *Spin* issue so profoundly disappointing was that there was no meaningful political edge to it. It evoked an easy, mainstream Black solidarity. There was a gathering of many Black voices, yet one had no sense of the writers' political orientations, of their political identities.

CW In some ways the interview with Al Sharpton exemplifies your point. One sees portrayed in that interview Sharpton's own sense of sacrificial engagement with Black struggle, so one admires and appreciates Sharpton because he is willing to die for Black folk, but on the other hand, you have to bring serious critique to bear on Sharpton because he does not actively incorporate critiques of capitalism, patriarchy, misogyny, and homophobia in his ideological project. His focus is primarily White supremacy and White supremacy needs criticism, needs resistance, and Sharpton is out there fighting it in his way, but he does not have an all inclusive vision or social analysis.

The late 1980s and early 1990s have seen a reemergence of Black activism. People are once again willing to put their lives on the line, which is very important, and an individual activist like Sharpton does live under the threat of death and we must never forget that. But on the other hand, there is a very real sense that someone like Sharpton does not have the wherewithal to project a sense of vision or the potential to provide effective leadership on a variety of issues. I say this not to degrade but to criticize from my own vantage point. These are the issues that made his interview so revealing.

bh One of the questions we as Black people have the most difficulty dealing with is our response to capitalism, and most particularly our lack of collective response to the way in which consumer capitalism has changed the nature of anything we could call Black life or Black experience. We want to act as though we have managed to hold on to traditional Black folk experience, with its ethical value system, while we participate wholeheartedly in consumer capitalism. We have been reluctant, as a people, to say that capitalism poses a direct threat to the survival of an ethical belief system in Black life.

CW Much of the nihilism in Black America and, it is true for America as a whole, is in part attributable to market forces, but by that, I also mean market mentalities that make people think the only way to achieve is to get over on someone else, to treat people as if they were simply objects hindering or benefitting one's own advancement.

We are enacting more and more a paradigm of market morality in which one understands oneself as living to consume, which in turn creates a market culture where one's communal and political identity is shaped by the adoration and cultivation of images, celebrityhood, and visibility as opposed to character, discipline, substantive struggle. And this is fundamentally transforming Black community in very ugly ways.

bh Cornel, it seems to me that one of the issues that keeps coming up in our critique of Black neo-nationalism and renewed Black liberation struggle is the evocation of icons without a sense of what kind of struggle must take place in order to carry out the mission of those icons.

The crucial issue for us is what we are going to do? Not how are we going to look, or what political slogan are we going to wear, but what forms of substantive struggle are we going to engage with our minds and bodies? I think there is a real loss of a sense of what to do. To be a people without an immediate sense of direction aggravates already present feelings of powerlessness. This is probably the major factor in ever rising rates of Black addiction, the lack of ability to invest oneself in a project larger than oneself that brings with it recognition and feelings of self-valuation.

CW A market culture will promote and promulgate an addiction to stimulation, it will put forward the view that, in order to be alive, one needs stimulation and he/she who is most alive is the person who is most stimulated. You see bodily stimulation projected through the marketing of sexuality, the marketing of sexual stimulation as the major means by which we construct desire. Along with market forces there has also been a certain collapse of structures of meaning and structures of feeling, reinforcing the sense that the meaning of life resides only in what you produce. But what you conceptualize yourself being able to produce is being shaped by market forces, namely through forms of stimulation. Ironically the ancient truths, such as, only a life lived in love and care and service, now come back to us with a revolutionary content because the only way to effectively deal with addiction is through some form of conversion. But the only way people are converted is when they are convinced that people care for them, people love them, people believe in them such that they can begin to care for themselves, love themselves, and believe in themselves.

bh What is profoundly disturbing in Shelby Steele's book *The Content of our Character* is that he attempts to take from Black people the level of support offered by a liberal White population trying to be responsive to Black pain. He takes that support away by trivializing Black pain and suffering in order to collapse that suffering with self-serving victimization. Now, you and I would be the first to acknowledge that in all communities there are going to be those people who will embrace victimization as a means of not assuming accountability for their lives. But to collapse, as Steele does, self-serving victimization with the lived pain and suffering of unemployment, poverty, addiction, AIDS, homelessness, and police brutality as though those two forms of despair are the same thing, is to invite a kind of mass myopia on the part of the dominant culture. This ideological standpoint invites one to say that the intensity of Black suffering is irrelevant because it is, in fact, nothing but a fashionable cop-out, an indolent desire to receive something for nothing.

CW Shelby Steele's text has, at the psychological level, a few insights. Unfortunately, it can be easily appropriated in a very insidious way by conservative forces in this society. The very notion of being a victim becomes something that is taboo. The very idea that we can talk about the Black American past and present independently of victimization is ridiculous. Yet, we can certainly talk about victimization without solely viewing ourselves as victims. Now Steele wants to make the latter point while denying the former and thereby our very real economic, social, political, and sexual victimization, which is the cause of so much of Black suffering, drops out of the picture.

bh What is both amazing and fascinating about his work is the way it seeks to remove the onus of accountability from Whiteness and White power structures, and it is this removal which is strange and new in current criticism. From slavery on, Black people have had to appeal to those White people with a moral sensibility which would allow them to acknowledge responsibility and seek to make reparations for the evils visited upon us. For someone like him to come along and say there is no such thing as assuming accountability for Black pain is morally dangerous. He must appeal to the contemporary White sensibility simply by virtue of his willingness to deny the historical significance of reparations.

CW What happens is that he has such an either-or view of the world that as soon as we begin talking about victimization, it makes us look as though we are somehow absolving Black people of responsibility, agency, and ambition. While what we are trying to do is historically situate that agency and responsibility within the context Black people find themselves—often circumstances not of their own choosing and in many ways beyond their control. So the individual makes a difference, yes, but never a difference independent of the context which produced that person.

bh Yet, despite his trivialization of Black pain, he does recognize that Black people have been traumatized and psychically wounded. This is something we cannot discuss enough at this historical moment. Because what we are also witnessing right now are the ravages of our not having attended collectively to the multi-layered psychic wounds of racism, wounds that take the form, as Steele points out, of paranoia, of being unable to even know when someone is actually against you or when you imagine they are against you. But again, unlike Steele, I see that to be one of the consequences of racist victimization, that your ability to grasp reality is distorted and perverted, yet I also do not see that as a psychic space which we choose to inhabit.

CW We have always had to deal with traumatization, but we have had buffers. We have had Black civil society, Black family, Black churches, Black schools, Black sororities and so forth. What market forces have done in the last twenty-five years is to thoroughly weaken those institutions of Black civil society so that dealing with the traumatization becomes more difficult because we have less to draw from. Our buffers have been weakened and we become more deracinated, we become more denuded, which means we become culturally naked. And for a downtrodden people to become culturally naked is to live in a kingdom of nothingness.

bh At what stage of racial integration and our participation in the prevailing economy did we, in fact, begin to look upon goods as the solace for psychic pain? Partially, any analysis of the place of addiction in Black life has to begin not with substances like alcohol and drugs but really with consumer goods.

For so long, Black folks have felt that our longing for goods is a justifiable longing because the desire for material well-being is the crux of the American dream. Every "American" is seeking a nice car, a nice place to live. However, the danger of this logic resides in the overvaluation of goods which leads to forms of consumption similar to addiction.

We deal with White supremacist assault by buying something to compensate for feelings of wounded pride and self-esteem. When we don't receive racial respect we try to regain feelings of worth through class competition and material possession. Goods function as an equalizer, allowing a person to falsely believe that there is opportunity through consumer choice. We also don't talk enough about food addiction alone or as a prelude to drug and alcohol addiction. Yet, many of us are growing up daily in homes where food is another way in which we comfort ourselves.

Think about the proliferation of junk food in Black communities. You can go to any Black community and see Black folks of all ages gobbling up junk food morning, noon, and night. I would like to suggest that the feeling those kids are getting when they're stuffing Big Macs, Pepsi, and barbecue potato chips down their throats is similar to the ecstatic, blissful moment of the narcotics addict. So if we want to talk about dealing with addiction in Black communities we are going to have to talk about consumption on all levels, the construction of desire, and the problems of unmediated, unfulfilled desire.

I remember myself as a young woman—and I think many Black folks who have grown up in materially underprivileged homes have experienced variations of this—after I left home and was earning a real salary for the first time, whenever I felt bad I would seek solace by buying a new outfit. Buying something gave me some measure of agency and consolation. We try to fulfill our needs and longings with material goods because buying is the only legitimate means by which this culture allows one to acknowledge or fulfill emotional needs. Even the new self-help culture springing up around us is predicated on purchasing the right book or being able to afford the right kind of therapy.

Many Black women of all ages talk jokingly about their "secret" shopping addiction. What they don't examine is that, despite however successful, powerful, and beautiful we are, we still carry a desperate inner longing for a sense of well-being, a sense of worth and respect so frequently denied us in this society.

CW Yes, this is at the center of the dilemma Black people find themselves in today: we have become the walking wounded, the psychically assaulted. The fundamental addiction is an addiction to status, an addiction to visibility precisely because Black people have been invisible. We have been nameless and are now in quest of a name recognition. Jesse Jackson's statement speaks for most of Black America when he says, "I am somebody." We've got to say this over and over again because its embodiments have been so thoroughly assaulted. We are addicted to status which means—and this is true for our middle-class and our Black leadership—we will do anything for status.

bh If Black leadership is hungry for name recognition, think about how this affects the underclass, we are so status conscious that people can manifest feelings of worthlessness for not owning the right brand of sneakers, feelings so perverted by political and economic powerlessness that murder can be justified in pursuit of the right status symbol, e.g. a pair of sneakers. People are out there saying to themselves that the only way to experience themselves as alive and valuable is by having this symbol, making what they do to get that symbol irrelevant.

One of the things Michael Dyson talks about is how this is actually the quintessential expression of capitalist entrepreneurism, where one understands the American dream as the will to do whatever it takes to acquire resources for individual enhancement because one's notion of identity is dependent on the ability to control one's public and private representation.

When thinking about addiction and intervention, we must remember that crack/cocaine addiction is new to Black life; consequently we have so few mechanisms in place, particularly as it affects the Black underclass. Where does one send a young Black man who's poor, who's crack-addicted in this society? Where do we go for healing? How do we begin to address his needs, the needs of any addicted individual? These crucial questions are still difficult for us to answer, yet, given the many treatment centers and methods White people can avail themselves of, why are we not creating Afro-centric paradigms and locations for recovery?

Let us also note that Black people "fortunate" enough to enter White-run recovery programs frequently suffer from racist discrimination and persecution in those centers which makes the question of Black recovery even more urgent.

One problem I foresee a Black recovery movement having to address is narrow Black nationalism currently advocated in popular culture which insists on confusing self-determination with separatism. A Black owned and operated facility does not necessarily mean that in the midst of White supremacy the politics that inform how that facility is run, how the individuals in that facility are cared for, actually critically intervene on the forces of colonization that attack us. We cannot be so myopic as to see something as just, simply because it is funded by Blacks and run by Blacks. Separatism without a political agenda is not Black self-determination.

CW I agree, but we can only make relative judgement, which is to say that we make judgement about something like a Black health care facility or Black day-care center relative to what the alternatives are at the moment. So we must not collapse self-determination and separatism while at the same time recognizing that it is better to have a problematic Black facility than no Black facility, or one that is denigrating the identity of Black folks. In the same way that it is better to have Spike Lee's Forty Acres and a Mule than to not have it, even though it is deserving of so many serious criticisms on so many different levels. We as a people so often have our backs up against the wall, and so much staring-down-our-throats, with so little reward or relief, signs of hope must be highlighted.

bh If we want signs of hope, we can look critically and analytically at the Sixties as a time of powerful transformation, even as we see its weaknesses. That to me would seem like a worthwhile project. That kind of critical interrogation could be crucial in furthering our understanding of Black self-determination and its relationship to critical consciousness so that it empowers people to fight for the transformation of the status quo. What disturbs me about the endorsement of Black capitalism since the late 1970s as a legitimate method of Black struggle and achievement is the reluctance of Black people to engage in any critiques of capitalism today. By supporting Black capitalism, we are continually endorsing the economic structures which are actively engaged in destabilizing Third World communities abroad and Black Americans in the United States.

Our ability to make healthy choices has also been impaired by capitalist media campaigns. It's at the point now where a Black woman might choose to spend her remaining dollars on relaxer rather than the condoms which could save her life.

CW There is a problem in talking about capitalism *per se* because it becomes a kind of abstraction where we can too easily locate blame. And, given present international political reality, in which it is so very difficult to envision credible, non-capitalist alternatives, simply critiquing capitalism will not bring us to higher ground. The question then becomes how do we promote non-market values such as equality, justice, love, care, and sacrifice in a society, culture, and world in which it is almost impossible to conceive of a non-capitalist alternative?

Here we learn from Elijah Muhammad; we have to acknowledge and support the expansion of the entrepreneurial class. Since we must have access to capital for survival, it becomes imperative that the Earl Graves and others be *critically* supported. They have to be able to use their profits and constitute their businesses in such a way that they are influenced and moved to communal accountability by non-market values. What do I mean by this? I mean they can still make profits, but they then could channel an appropriate portion of those profits into Black community development. They still have businesses, but investment decisions are more cooperative than hierarchical. Because, as Elijah understood, it is a struggle to make real non-capitalist ventures in American society.

bh Carol Stack, a White woman anthropologist, wrote a book entitled *All Our Kin,* which was a study of kinship structures among poor Black people. She wrote the book within a capitalist context but she was documenting oppositional values mediating in the community. Those values demanded that individuals with resources share those resources in such a way that the wealth, however relative that wealth was in a given community, not be situated solely in the hands of one individual or one household.

So when we talk about how African Americans have changed, it is that we now have fewer visions of how to keep alive a sense of community in the midst of struggle.

Now I, for example, currently have a middle-class life.

CW In terms of material existence. Yes, that's true for both of us.

bh Yet, I'm part of a family and community of Black people whose lives do not have the level of material comfort that I am able to have in my individual life. Given this reality, what is my responsibility to those who are less materially fortunate than me? What are the limits of my responsibility in relation to family? As Black people from the 1960s and 1970s with a greater potential, relatively speaking, for upward mobility, we have not answered these questions. So we have a burgeoning Black middle class, devoid of Black civic institutions, and inclusive Black community who see upward mobility as a severing of family connection, if family connections are not middle-class connections. The Black middle class has become increasingly exclusive, desperately protective of its "piece of the pie," meaning that we would rather safeguard our money than extend helping hands to our families. Perhaps the Black middle class is at the point where we should begin to attempt reinscribing some of those values of sharing and service that seem so deeply lost to us now.

CW Ironically enough, though, we can learn something from the new narrow Black nationalist renaissance. For example, if you listen to music from the 1970s as opposed to music from the 1980s, the latter, despite its narrow rhetoric, emphasizes sharing and caring for others, as well as highlighting the plight of those who are disadvantaged. These lyrics indicate both a need and potential readiness for a cultural renaissance. A transformation of values that could eventually evolve into renewed organizations, revived organizations or new organizations and, most importantly, maybe a new cadre of leadership. Much of what we're talking about has not just to do with the nihilism in the Black community—meaninglessness is rampant—but that we don't have leaders who can really convince people to believe in themselves. Partly this is so because they are caught up within a system that does not allow current leaders to speak with a power that affirms the very people they claim to be concerned about. This is new in the Black community. Given the circumstances of segregation, our leaders had to be able to not simply speak a language of narrow liberal public policy or conservative public policy; they had to speak a language of spirituality which empowered a downtrodden people. Now what you get is either the policy analysts or the rhetoric of politicians concerned with the same things all politicians are concerned with, winning the next election and gaining money from the lobbyists. So we have a vacuum. And what is interesting about the Al Sharptons, the Farrakhans, and whole hosts of others who have tried to fill the vacuum, is that they recognize that there is a level which is not being reached or touched or tapped by Black politicians.

This is also why many in the contemporary Black middle class do not understand its moral responsibility to the working-class, and why Black individuals with economic privilege identify deracination as the mark of success.

bh I would add Shahrazad Ali to your list of current self-proclaimed leaders.

CW Very much so. In fact, her book speaks in some ways more directly to these questions than Farrakhan or Sharpton.

bh Her book is antithetical to many of the values we are talking about. It is anti-service and anti-sharing, values most clearly manifested when she advocates that Black men not pay child support, that they keep the money and spend it themselves.

There is a deep and profound correlation between a book like the *Black Man's Guide to Understanding the Black Woman* and Shelby Steele's *The Content of our Character*. Both of these books envision the family in patriarchal individualist terms; both books envision the male as family leader and primary household provider. This vision is dangerously ahistorical. Furthermore, we are seeing that this model does not work for White people, and many of them are, at this historical moment, coming to terms with the failure of the patriarchal model to truly sustain the family. If we look at the rise in domestic violence in White families, the condemnation of marital rape, date rape, and incest, all of these things are an indication to us that the White supremacist patriarchal family structure as we have historically known it is collapsing in on itself, has been destructive from its inception. It seems always ironic and painful that conservative Black people who want to constitute themselves as spokespeople like Steele and Ali, in fact, are taking that model and suggesting to us as Black people that we can somehow redeem ourselves with it. When you think of that last line in Ali's book, "Rise Black man, take your rightful place as ruler of the universe," it evokes a fascistic, autocratic rule which has been responsible for the most horrific institutions of repression of the last five centuries—slavery, pogroms, concentration camps, genocide of indigenous people—and of which we are now witnessing a slow ideological and material collapse.

We would do well as Black people to note with what frequency White people now utilize mass media to, in fact, promote notions of equal partnership within White family life. We see dozens of White sitcoms, soap operas, and feature-length films which have the working wife and the "househusband," the domestically sensitized man of the Eighties. These representations have been preparing White people to accept the complexity of contemporary gender relationships. White America appears to be very concerned with opening up the arena of gender relations, where women and men can freely say the old paradigms aren't working anymore. So it is frightening to know that it is a White power structure that is promoting a Shelby Steele, a Shahrazad Ali, because it certainly isn't Black people who are putting Ali on the Donahue, Heraldo, and Sally Jesse Raphael shows.

As cultural critics, we wonder what interest White media establishment has in advancing the notion that the perceived and tangible failures in Black life are a failure of Black men to achieve effective patriarchal control. Why do White people want to perpetuate the myth of Black men rising through the subordination of Black women? We must interrogate these messages coming to us via Black people, when we know that White establishment perceives loving family and effective community to be the most potent formula for conducting effective resistance to tyranny.

CW In the case of Shahrazad Ali, you also have something else going on. She becomes, in the eyes of Black men, an antidote to their image of Black feminism.

bh Absolutely.

CW The image foremost in their minds is a kind of vulgar reading of *The Color Purple,* in which the Black man is the brutal misogynist. Suddenly you have a Black woman ardently sympathetic to their cause, as it were. This then goes hand-in-hand with the narrow Black nationalist renaissance because nationalism, any form of nationalism, is usually a profoundly sexist endeavor, albeit an empowering one for a group in society which is cast in solely negative images, which in this case is the Black man. So Ali, independent of Donahue and Company, would still flourish in the Black community.

bh Yes, but the Black community was not reading the Reaganite George Gilder's *Wealth and Poverty.* And yet he was saying many of the same things Ali is saying. So what I am trying to do is expose the link between the conservatism of a Black nationalism that seeks to reinscribe patriarchy and the White power structure, while completely agreeing with you that Ali's work also has its own very specific context within autonomous Black community. Black men in this culture feel collectively unable to articulate the myriad ways in which they have been ravaged by this system, and

Ali comes forward to speak, in a reactionary and divisive way, to the reality of Black male pain.

CW That's right. That is what you see with Ishmael Reed, one of our great literary talents, and an intense conservative when it comes to sexual politics. So we have these men bitterly complaining that Black male pain is thoroughly overlooked by Black feminists, and here comes Ms. Ali to confirm their ideas as a Black woman. How does she do this? By casting Black male pain as being caused by Black woman's empowerment. So what you get is Black men and women on the same leaky boat floating in the larger capitalist and White supremacist context, but now we have license to be at each other's throats during the journey. I wonder how many of us will get off the boat, ready to withstand and resist that capitalist, White supremacist context?

bh If we look at the seminal work, however problematic it is, *Black Macho and the Myth of the Superwoman* by Michele Wallace, which also sold more than any other book by a Black feminist…

CW You mean non-fiction book.

bh Yes, a book of feminist social critique. If we look at Michele Wallace's work in relation to Shahrazad Ali's, we see that Ali's invokes a narrow sexist Black nationalism in the same way that Wallace's book represented a narrow radical feminism that refused to address male pain. And at that historical moment, feminist movement dominated by White women was saying that the most important mission was to acknowledge the sexism of men. And to some extent, the purpose of *Black Macho* was to compel Black people to acknowledge the sexism in Black life, and, unfortunately, that was done at the expense of discussing the ways in which Black men are potentially victimized and traumatized by patriarchy. In this sense, certainly, Michele Wallace has herself critiqued that particular strand of analysis in *Black Macho.* Yet this is the image of Black feminism that continues to linger in the minds of Black people. That Black feminism is first and foremost an attack upon the Black man, not an attack upon sexism, because sexism does not appear to enter into the debate, but an attack upon the Black man by the Black woman as agent acting in collusion with White men and women against the Black man.

Harlem Nights and *Mo' Better Blues* carried images of a careerist Black, symbolic of what we might see as a liberated Black woman. Yet these women are seen as betrayers, women who betray men in the interest of their own advancement.

Why isn't there a growing number of feminist scholars who are intervening on these perceptions? As a feminist critic, to what degree am I accountable for intervening on negative representations?

One of the major changes I see in my own work over the last ten years is that I am addressing much more directly Black community and Black life. Feminist theory does not emerge as a discourse rooted in any kind of discussion of Blackness, so to some extent, Black women, like myself, who entered that discourse did not enter it through the door of gender, race, and class. We came to it in terms of gender alone and have been struggling ever since for recognition of race and class.

The question preoccupying me now is, how do we talk about sexism in Black life? My essay "Black Men: Reconstructing Black Masculinity" is a very different essay from "The Imperialism of Patriarchy" in *Ain't I a Woman*. This difference reflects ten years of development in my own critical, theoretical consciousness. And now I see what I did not see as a young woman studying and developing intellectually in predominantly White institutions: that if we want to seriously intervene on destructive tendencies in the Black community, then we have to produce texts and narratives that directly address the issues confronted by Black communities.

CW I agree, but as critics we must also ask what audience we will be reaching. More important than brief television slots like the Arsenio Hall show or the Oprah Winfrey show are organizations and groups which provide public and private forums for debate. One of the reasons prophetic Black churches are so very important is because they are one of the few remaining public spheres where ideas can be discussed and disseminated among ordinary people who are struggling with these issues in their everyday lives. Many people would prefer to take the easy route which is relying solely on TV for information and debate. These people believe that high-profile visibility achieves effective communication and change without ever organizing at the grassroots level. We have to move in both directions—televisual and grassroots. On the grassroots level, we ensure potential change, and on the televisual level, we broadcast quickly and in abbreviated form information regarding social movements.

bh Writing has been the primary medium through which issues of gender are publicly discussed on all levels of Black community life, with the most catalytic texts being *Black Macho, The Color Purple,* and *Black Man's Guide*. Yet these discussions are not subversive, critically intervening, or theoretically sophisticated. In fact, more than anything else, they have become public spectacle, representing and reinforcing the spirit of divisiveness between Black men and Black women. On the one hand, more Black women are beginning to talk about sexism, are beginning to identify themselves as victims of male domination in various arenas of their lives. The *Black Women's Health Book* edited by Evelyn White signals the impact and power of White, feminist self-recovery movement as a way of bringing Black women to consciousness once those theoretical principles are transposed onto a Black context. Black women are trying to establish a healthier foundation from which to assert agency. To which Black men respond by saying, in effect, the degree to which Black women assert agency is the degree to which I am kept down.

CW That is the tragedy I was speaking about when I said we had license to be at each other's throats. Unfortunately, in North American society, one of the major means by which Black men are empowered is to have power over Black women. For a people who feel already relatively powerless, it becomes a form of competition to not occupy the bottom rung of the ladder. We see this in relation to Black American color caste and we see it in relation to gender. The question is how do we sever Black male notions of empowerment from requiring the active subordination of Black women? It is not only the Black male that has subordinated Black women. The Black woman has been subordinated by White and non-White elites in almost every society where Black women live. So how do we make the majority of Black men disinvest from a definition of power which requires subordination of Black women? We have to have reflections on Black male agency that are healthy and empowering in a substantive way. We must have a way of conceptualizing and enacting codes of behavior that are in the interest of the Black community. What we are witnessing instead is the Black community is becoming both a wasteland and a combat zone. Our only way out of this vicious syndrome of disenfranchised despair is to have new leadership that resists those individuals and structures that use power to subordinate and subjugate.

bh Historically, when gender strife has arisen between Black men and women, particularly Black heterosexual men and women, there has been the sense that, despite disagreements, it was important to maintain loving bonds, loving connection with one another. This ethics of mutual care can be seen in the lyrics of that time as well. Otis Redding's "This is My Lover's Prayer, I Hope It Reaches

Out to You My Love," is a good example of the humanity we are talking about. A song that simultaneously collapses mutual objectification with consumer mentality is "Nothing Going On but the Rent." This song's message stands in total opposition to the message of older Black music which invoked a Black romantic bonding which was invested in locating avenues or reconciliation for circumstances in which we have wronged each other .

CW That is very true. We were listening earlier today to Kenneth Gamble and Leon Huff. In "The Jones Girl," the lyrics go, "There will not be peace on Earth until man makes peace with Woman." Gamble and Huff, though talking about a patriarchal family, they made a call for reconciliation.

I must say, though, when we listen closely to the lyrics of two of the finest producers in the country today, namely, L.A Reid and Babyface, you do get a Black womanist sensibility on behalf of Black women. If you listen to "Superwoman" and a host of their songs, you find, in fact, a critique of Black male patriarchy. Even though it is still predominantly a call for romantic love. There is no doubt that Babyface is deeply tied to a romantic love ethic. So there are signs of hope, and maybe we ought to turn to some of the signs of hope because they seem to be so few these days.

bh Well, I wanted us to talk a bit about this. I see the gender strikes between Black men and women as being completely enhanced by Shahrazad Ali's book.

I was in an African store in New York and two Black men were standing there describing to one another how it is important to hit Black women in the mouth. Without a doubt, the most dangerous message of the *Black Man's Guide to Understanding the Black Woman* is the advocation of the use of physical violence to control, subdue and subordinate Black women. When I think about that I think that Ali isn't really coming up with this ideology herself. She is mirroring the ideology that is already at work within various Black communities of all classes. We should also make it clear that the problem of Black patriarchal domination is the problem of all Black classes. It is not solely a problem of the Black underclass. It seems to me, Cornel, that the situation is very grave because it is a distortion of the notion of romantic love to want to see obedience as the quintessential expression of respect. Part of what certain sectarian forms of Islam, certain forms of narrow Afrocentric thinking advocate is obedience, particularly obedience of the woman to the man. In part, we have to talk about how do we begin to rethink our notions of heterosexual bonding, our notions of respect. One of the things I value in our friendship, our political bonding, is the sense that we respect one another in the fullness of our beings. That I respect you for your intellectual commitments, your spiritual commitments, your ethical beliefs. What I've been thinking a lot about is through what vehicles might we transmit that way of thinking about bonding between Black men and women to a larger group of Black people.

CW Here lies the challenge. Here we have to be very critical of leftists like ourselves, who find it very easy to rethink and reconceptualize, but so very difficult to live out our critiques on a daily basis. For example, after critiquing the patriarchal family, what kind of relations are there? How do we actually live those relations? Because people are interested in new ways of life, not just new ways of thinking.

bh Talk about it.

CW What new ways of life can we credibly present to others in terms of our own moral example? Now, on the one hand, we do know Black egalitarian family relations, not too many, but there are some. Now what goes into these relationships? What made these people not only rethink but commit themselves to a new way of life?

We need organizations that exemplify to people on an everyday basis what can be done in terms of new families, new churches, de-patriarchalized churches. What would a Black church look like without patriarchy? What would a Black family look like?

bh One of the things that was a joy for me when we were both teaching at Yale was worshipping at the Black church at Yale. And the thing I liked most about the sermons was the emphasis on anti-sexism, the emphasis on rethinking and reinterpreting scripture in a manner that would not reinscribe and reinforce patriarchy. Dwight Andrews gave particularly meaningful and progressive sermons on Mother's Day. He would try to look anew at particular scriptures and see how Christianity upholds the dignity of women, how it can uphold the dignity of women when it is not being used in the service of patriarchy.

It is a new thing, in a sense, for us as Black intellectuals to try and take on the issue of gender in such a way that we are not just trying to communicate with our books but communicating through our behavior in daily life. These issues go beyond the politically correct lip service.

I was not prepared when you and I first spoke together at the Yale African American cultural center for the number of people who came to me to say that this was the first time in their lives they had seen a Black man and a Black woman have this kind of dialogue together. And this confirms something I tell my students: "If you can't imagine something, it can't come into being." But even more, I think, the most powerful impact that we had that day was not even so much the words we said but the manner in which we conducted ourselves—two individuals in solidarity.

7

Dialogue Between bell hooks and Cornel West

You see, the fact is we're too close to the horrors of the ghetto to ever romance about it...The negro mother really would rather have a tuberculosisless baby—than even the mighty Blue's! That's one of the secrets of our greatness as a people; legends to the contrary, we do have our feet on this green earth. Oh yes, darlin'! Our spiritual affirmation of life rests on a most materialistic base. How else could we come up with a song like "Oh, Lord, I Don't Feel Noways Tired!"

No—I said—don't you worry about us, child. We know where we're going and we know how we're going to get there. And I started to tap my foot a little, thinking of the song I'd just mentioned and its triumphant spirit. Oh, yes! It's going to come gently and beautiful, like the sweetness of our old folkways; going to spill out and over the world from our art like the mighty waves of a great spiritual.

Lorraine Hansberry
Young, Gifted, and Black

bh Returning to the subject of Spike Lee, let's talk about the impact he has on young Black people. I went to see *Mo' Better Blues* in a theater with a predominantly Black audience. Outside the theater were young Black girls and boys between the ages of eleven and sixteen asking if they could come in with us. It is undeniable that this age group, between ten and eighteen, is deeply influenced by cinema in their understanding of relationships. If you look at our childhood, we were influenced by what we saw at church. We weren't influenced by seeing Black relationships in the media because there were none.

CW Yes, our role models were in the neighborhood, church, and within our own families.

bh Working with young Black people, I see more and more that even within our own families we are not seeing adult Black men and women talking with each other. We see instead Black men and women talking at one another, across one another, giving orders, making demands, but not really having a conversation. One aspect of *Mo' Better Blues* that really disturbed me and could have been altered so easily was Bleek returning to Indigo and saying, "Save my life." It was similar to the moment in *Harlem Nights* when the Black man turns to the Black woman and says, "Help me to be the best self I can be; help me to self-actualize." But instead of talking to each other, exploring their individual and mutual pain, verbalized pain becomes a precursor to sex. Bleek did not feel the need to, for one thing, tell her where he had been for one year, what happened to him, ask what had been happening with her, etc. So again the question of process is discarded, communicative intimacy is replaced with superficial sex.

CW Naturally, I believe one only asks one person to save one's life and that is the savior. So any time you cast a human being, especially a woman, as savior, you are asking that person to engage in a level of sacrifice which will more than likely be manipulated by the person who is asking.

Now, thirty seconds after coming through the door, Bleek is carrying her upstairs and is most likely on top of her a few seconds after that. So she is no longer savior. She is being subordinated, as well as engaging in pleasure production. So that when he's asking her to save his life, it is nothing more than typical patriarchal manipulation.

When Bleek's back is against the wall, he sees his options as either putting a woman up on a pedestal as savior to be subordinated and manipulated, or she must be abused violently.

bh And that violence is what we see in *Harlem Nights*. One of the most tragic visions of Black heterosexuality I have seen in contemporary Black American cinema. Imagine, the Black man and woman make love to one another and then one of them murders the other. Talk about a violation of our sense of the sacred. If we talk about sex as a metaphor for offering and sharing oneself, we see those two characters genuinely sharing themselves before sex and yet they are still prepared to and capable of doing one another in after the act of genuine sharing. Is this Black love, tragic and bleak? Who are we producing this vision for? I thought a great deal about that.

Eddie Murphy is a very different character from Spike Lee. We see that in *Raw* which is a real evocation of a pugilistic eroticism. When Murphy says, "A woman doesn't want you to tell her that you love her, she wants to be fucked to death." We can't get a more violent sense of eroticism, a more anti-body politic.

CW And anti-human.

bh Anti-life, fundamentally. And the thing that I find fascinating is that so many of these messages are coming to us from young Black men. Black men who haven't even had the opportunity in life to experience deep and profound romantic relationships. Think of Murphy as a man in his twenties making *Raw,* as a man gaining celebrity and wealth through image production. How responsible and experienced can we expect this young man to be with the images he chooses to create?

We are accountable as well because we have to talk among ourselves as Black people about what a relationship is. However flawed Haki Madhabuti's book *Black Men* is, it heralds a historical moment when there are Black folks, Black nationalists, Black Afrocentric thinkers who are trying to confront the reality of sexism. One of the sweet sections of *Black Men* is where he tells us that Black men can no longer expect Black women to go out and work all day and come home and "service" their needs, either their domestic needs or their sexual needs. And it is amazing that at such a point of critical breakthrough—and I do see this as a critical breakthrough in Afro-centric thinking—we would have a book like Ali's, which literally beats Madhubuti's book down. And to have that notion visually reinforced when Ali beat down Madhubuti's way of thinking about Black masculinity, his urging of Black men to rethink who they are in the world, on the Donohue show. This was very, very painful to watch because I see some Black men as trying to open up a discourse on gender and sexuality, and they are not receiving the attention, respect, and recognition one would hope for. Black men like yourself and Madhabuti are trying to assume accountability for sexism, are trying to say that the violence can no longer continue, that it is no longer acceptable.

CW It is very interesting that we would continually allude to films and popular culture because, when we look at literature and the various perceptions of how male characters respond to relationships within literature, we see primarily Black men and White women. One reason for this could be that, in popular culture, interracial relationships are still too controversial, the potential profit margin is not guaranteed. So we don't see interracial relationships depicted, yet we know Black men "escape" these kinds of problems with Black women by sometimes genuinely, sometimes inauthentically falling in love with White women.

Take the early novels of John Wideman, for example, where the Black intellectual is continually interacting with White women, trying to come to terms with himself and White women. And how, in fact, that impinges on the very reality that we are talking about, interracial relationships.

bh If we critically and analytically examine Black male and White female relationships, we will find that all too often the Black men who are in those relationships are buying into very patriarchal, sexist notions of virgin/whore. That is to say, seeing White woman as symbolic of a more innocent, less aggressive expression of womanhood. And if one juxtaposes this sexist notion with Shahrazad Ali's insistence that the Black woman is aggressive, demanding, verbal, one realizes how easily one has bought right into the operative mythology surrounding White femininity as embodying submissiveness, unassertiveness, purity.

It is important for us to interrogate interracial relationships on that level rather than on a more superficial level which would simplistically label any Black man with a White woman as non-Black identified. It seems to me much more interesting to talk about how Black men who buy into conventional sexist and patriarchal ways of thinking seem to be the best candidates for also buying into the notion that White women symbolize a different kind of femininity and womanhood. I think, for example, of the *New York Woman* article that Brent Peters did entitled "The White Girl Problem." He essentially talks about the anger he, as a Black man, gets from Black women who see him with White women. Yet what also becomes clear in the piece is his complete lack of interest in Black women.

I would ask if any Black man on this planet is truly interested in himself if he is not interested in Black women, and this does not necessarily mean he has to exclusively befriend, date, or marry Black women. There is no reason for a Black man who has chosen an individual White partner to not still extend his care, kindness, and consideration to Black women. Yet, we often see just the opposite. I can't tell you how many times Black women tell me that they've written some Black man off because he's with a White woman. Now hearing this, superficially would lead one to think, oh, the Black woman is yet again expressing her anger, rage, jealousy towards White women. Yet what is really being evoked is the pain of negation.

When I walk down the street and I see a Black man with a White woman and he looks me eye-to-eye with respectful recognition, I don't feel betrayed. I don't feel like his choice is necessarily informed by a disdain for Blackness, but if he ignores me, then I think the brother has got a problem with self-love, self-imaging, and racial identity.

CW I agree. I'm thinking of the late great St. Clair Drake who was exogamously married but who had an interest in Black men and women more evident than most Black men married to Black women. I can also say that about a few close friends of mine who are exogamously married and, yet, at the same time, I do believe that deep down in the depths of the Black male psyche is a struggle with taking seriously the beauty of Black women. The ideals of White beauty, when it comes to women, are so deeply inscribed in every male psyche, Black and White, that many brothers do have problems acknowledging Black beauty, and by beauty I don't simply mean physical beauty.

One of the things that is reflected in growing up in a Black community is being attuned to a certain styles and mannerisms that one defines as attractive and desirable. In a way, I would argue it is a gift from my childhood that in growing up within a Black community, I could be profoundly attracted to certain styles Black women have. Now in some senses this is arbitrary because someone else may have grown up in a White neighborhood and learned those styles to be negative. But if one does learn to see those styles as attractive, then that is a way to understanding what is beautiful about Black women physically and stylistically. This is something I see many brothers having trouble with.

bh I would go deeper, Cornel, and say it starts with the trouble Black men have with themselves. I have a long standing crush, from a distance, on Kareem Abdul Jabar, and one of the things that I like from his autobiographical writings is that he's been so deeply honest about how he saw himself and his own physicality. If we look at Black athletes like Michael Jordan, we assume that this person who we are seeing in his magnificence sees himself as magnificent, but what we know is that all too often in this society Black men who are tall and well-built, Black men who might have large penises, don't see themselves as wonderful and magnificent but, in fact, see themselves as the embodiment of that which is most hated, most despised, and most unworthy in this society. So some Black men turn to White women seeking affirmation of the very Blackness that they can't affirm for themselves. Seeking the validation of White women because they have no inner sense of validation.

If you have a White woman on your arm telling you how much she loves your muscles then you can have a different relationship to your muscles and their worth in the greater White society. Part of the real anguish we are having as Black men and women is that Black men don't love their bodies. Even powerful Black men whose bodies have been part of what brings them fame and glory. They have not been able to take glory in their physicality because they are always perceived as threatening.

CW I think a significant number of Black men do view themselves as wonderful and magnificent, but only in certain spheres.

So, given the myth of Black male sexual prowess, they view themselves as being wonderful and magnificent in terms of how they interact with women. And in their construction of pleasure they have internalized the notion of White women as being the providers of a higher level of pleasure than Black women. That's a deep thing. Once a brother is locked into that he's sliding down a slippery slope, but many of us do because the myth is perpetuated every day.

The Last Poets used to talk about White thighs versus Black thighs, and they'd get into brothers dreaming about White thighs. I wonder how many of them dreamt about Black thighs. We are really getting vulgar, but we might as well get some of this out. In relation to the Last Poets, we are talking about this as a way in which pleasure is constructed in the Black male psyche.

bh Absolutely. When Alice Walker first wrote her story on pornography, "And You Can't Keep a Good Woman Down," many people objected. They said Black men don't read pornography, but, in fact, one of the things Kareem Abdul Jabar talks about in his autobiography is the pornographic magazines in his house.

CW When he was a child?

bh Yes, and that the body idealized in those magazines was the White female body.

CW Today, TV is, in many instances, pornographic, if one sees exploitative sexual objectification of the human body as a form of pornography. And the idealized sexual object remains the White woman.

bh In terms of the construction of Black femaleness in fashion magazines like *Vogue, Elle,* and *Mirabella,* often Black women's bodies are positioned in a freakish, distorted manner. Black women are put in unnatural wigs and shown in contorted positions so that the adjacent White female body always appears to be a signifier of "natural" beauty. The Black woman, on the other hand, is treated as this figure whose beauty is somehow constructed, artificial, devoid of inherent beauty. This is still a major issue for Black women in terms of the development of our sexual identities.

CW Aesthetics have substantial political consequences. How one views oneself as beautiful or not beautiful or desirable or not desirable has deep consequences in terms of one's feelings of self-worth and one's capacity to be a political agent. This is something Marcus Garvey understood. One of his great insights was the knowledge that aesthetic appearance had to be reversed before Black people could become full political agents. Again, the problem has to do with simplistic reversals. One can't simply have an inversion which is Black supremacy. Garvey himself never promoted Black supremacy, though Elijah did. But what we as a people need is a sincere appreciation of African Beauty that remains intact even as we interact with other peoples. So that we are able to affirm ourselves without putting others down. That is the sign of moral maturity.

bh It also means we have to deepen our understanding of beauty. To the extent that we have to learn that a self-loving Black person is infinitely more beautiful than a self-hating one. We dwell on the superficialities of skin color and hair texture without seeing that those are symptoms. How many light-skinned Black folks do we know who are steeped in a debilitating self-hatred, even though they are perceived as "more Beautiful" inside and outside the race? So one issue we face in rethinking Black liberation struggle is understanding that struggle as beginning with the self, as Toni Cade Bambara said in her essay "On the Issue of Roles," this involves a conversion of our notions of beauty.

Toni Morrison talks about how hurting it has been to us as a people to endure certain notions of beauty and perpetuate them and impose them. For example, most of the psychic pain many

Black men feel—and I think we see this acted out cinematically by Spike—has to do with feeling that they don't measure up to Black women's beauty ideals.

The prioritization of the physical at the expense of everything else allows a woman to believe that if you've got a man who doesn't look good, then you've got to be scamming on him for material goods. These kinds of value systems have produced a very corrupt vision of Black heterosexuality and Black relational bonding.

CW This difficulty of loving one's self makes it then difficult to be kind, considerate, and caring because when one is talking about relationships one is not simply talking about beauty in terms of love of the self. One is talking about a beauty that can be manifested in terms of how you treat your significant other, and how you take his or her needs and thoughts into consideration.

bh Which is what makes the ending of *Mo' Better Blues* so shallow—it is precisely all those things that are not taken into consideration. One of the painful things for me as a viewer was Lee's choice of "A Love Supreme" in that last scene when Coltrane's musical aim was to evoke precisely that high level of consideration, that care that is God-like and God-informed. Not a shallow notion of care, but a deep and profound sense of respect that is truly about looking at another person and recognizing what they need, what you can give to them to nurture their overall well-being, their spiritual, physical, emotional well-being. That sense of "A Love Supreme" was really about the combination of all of those forces, and it was a real movement away, if people know his career, from romantic notions of love that suggest love is not an act of will. Coltrane was really talking about that union with the divine that enables us to love more deeply and fully here on earth.

CW Yes, that is part of the genius of Coltrane in relation to his insights about life which are inseparable but not reducible to the genius of his music.

But let us backtrack to interracial relationships and Black women. This debate seems to become especially heated when the topic of professional Black women and the potential partners of professional Black women arises.

What about the issue of Black intellectual partners? Now, do you, for example, as a Black intellectual, have to have a significant other that is an intellectual, or what does it mean for a Black professional woman to be with a non-professional brother, or vice versa? Does a professional Black woman have to be with a professional Black man?

bh Well, focusing specifically on Black heterosexuals, I would say that it is very important to distinguish intellectuality from professionalism and being in a professional class. Although it is very important for me as an individual to be with an intellectual, it is not important to me to be with someone who is in a professional class.

CW Why is it important to be with an "intellectual"?

bh It is important to be with politically like-minded people. Now, when I use the term intellectual, I use it broadly. What I really mean is that I want to be with a critical thinker. We know there are many, many underclass Black folks, jobless folks, etc. who are critical thinkers, who have keen analytical abilities, so I would say it is crucial to be with critically engaged individuals. One of the things I find, Cornel, is that I feel truly blessed at this stage of my life with my work. I consider my work a gift given to me by the divine and I feel that one of the standards of my life that I am trying to abide by is that I cannot see myself partnered in companionship with anyone who did not have respect for that work and that process. I think what life often shows us is that it is very difficult for women to get someone to respect our working process who don't themselves have some understanding of that process. We have many examples of the intellectual man of all races who might be with a woman who doesn't even bother to read very much, but she may have profound awe and respect and want to be a supportive agent for that man. I don't think we have very many examples of a man wanting to be that supportive agent for a woman, especially if he feels that somehow he may not be able to have access to the process. So often, Black intellectual women end up desiring similar partners, people with similar processes who have that understanding. As long as we are within patriarchy, so much of gender relations is based on the notion of women in a service capacity. Take me, for example. Writing is an alone activity; I spend enormous amounts of time alone. How could I have a man in my life who thought that the role of the woman in the household would be to meet his every need? Part of the beauty of the long relationship I had with another Black male intellectual is that I never felt a lack of respect on his part for my need to go off alone and work. Feminism has not had a meaningful impact, I believe, on how we think about the daily politics of heterosexual relationships. There is a book called *The Second Shift* by a White woman sociologist who tells us that women are still doing most of the work in the home. The more educated the man is, the more work he thinks he is doing but is not really doing.

CW So the expectation remains, across class and race lines, that women will do the work?

bh Right. One of the things which distinguishes intellectual work from the work of being an academic is that intellectual work is not often confined. I lie in bed at night and think over theoretical problems I'm trying to work out. When I lived with my partner of fourteen years, many a night I would wake him up to say I have this idea running through my head about Black men and women under slavery, let me run it by you.

One of the sweet things I read about Arsenio Hall recently had him talking about why he doesn't have a committed relationship. He told an anecdote about having sex with a woman where they were being particularly loud when all of a sudden it occurred to him that the neighbors were saying, "Now you know he's not that good." Immediately a whole skit came to his mind and he had to get up out of bed and go off to work it out. So in order to have this kind of creative process, which is basically being creatively engaged twenty-four hours a day, you have got to be with someone who respects that process. Whether they actually utilize that process themselves or not is not as important as their respect for it.

CW Yes, but it doesn't strike me that one has to be an intellectual professional to respect that.

bh I totally agree.

CW But it seems to me you are making a stronger claim. You are saying that they have to have some understanding of what it is like to be in the midst of that process.

bh I'm saying that under patriarchy men are less likely to identify with women in that process.

CW That's true, very true. You hear over and over again how talented women are threatening and intimidating to men in general and Black men in particular. Therefore, I think you are right; under patriarchy it is more difficult for a highly talented woman to find someone who will both respect and understand her work process than it is for a professional man.

I've always had a feeling that there was a kind of double standard (I'm going to get in a lot of trouble saying this) of Black professional women who tended to almost exclude non-professional Black men who would respect what they were doing, who would be egalitarian, who would love them deeply.

bh Well, Cornel, in that instance we are talking about a certain kind of bourgeois Black woman who has a very conventional/conservative notion of relationships and politics. One of the things that I would say as a radical Black woman who feels that more Black women need to be engaged in Black feminist revolutionary thinking is that a book like Shahrazad Ali's gains notoriety precisely because part of the power of the book is that it hints at certain truths and, like Shelby Steele's book, wields those truths against us.

One of the major critiques she makes in *Black Man's Guide* is of the bourgeois woman who has an idealized notion of relationships, an idealized expectation of material goods, and who is status conscious. Those critiques are truly relevant. She names this woman as somebody who has been looking at White women on TV, from *Mary Tyler Moore* to *L.A. Law,* and deciding that this is what womanhood should be universally. The core of that dilemma is Black women rethinking, first of all, our own relation to Black womanhood so that we don't want to just be carbon copies of the middle-class or upper-class White woman. Media depictions of White romance lead us to idealize relationships not even based on real-life relationship with any man, but some kind of Cinderella myth where one constructs the idealized hero. It seems to me that professional Black women who are trapped in those kinds of idealizations make it impossible for themselves to have an authentic relationship with a Black man or any man.

CW Here again reality comes in. Can we, in fact, live our lives after we have put forward our critiques of prevailing institutions like the family and so forth? How does a radical Black woman actually live her life outside of possible isolation, loneliness, and solitude if, after these thorough-going critiques, there are no brothers out there? No brothers who can engage in egalitarian relationships, no brothers who can respect her process, no brothers who understand their own process. Are they then simply living lives alone and providing us with these powerful critiques, while they themselves are not able to reach the fulfillment that they deserve?

bh I think two relational options that many Black women have not considered in the past that have now come to the fore are: one, relationships with White men and men of other ethnicities; and, two, relationships with women. I think there are multiple reasons why people lead lesbian-identified lives. There are women who will tell you they were born lesbians, but I also see a group of women, many of whom may have been married, who have children, who basically see themselves as bisexual or who may have seen themselves as completely heterosexual but got tired of loneliness and romantic isolation while they were waiting to have these "great" relationships with men. Those are two relational options that more and more Black women are opening themselves up to. Precisely because we don't want to live the rest of our lives alone.

To my mind, *The Color Purple* was the first fictional work to explicitly bring this possibility to the·fore.

CW In terms of popular culture?

bh Yes. And I think it really shook many Black people up. I think many Black people resented the relationship between Shug and Celie. We certainly see the extreme attack on Black lesbianism in Shahrazad Ali's book, where she wants to argue that all lesbians are really trying to be Black men. Which in fact denies that for many Black women, choosing to love another Black woman is really not about being anti-male at all but participating in a kind of celebratory rejoicing in one's womanness. This is what I think Walker tried to exemplify in *The Color Purple*: that it is actually in her relationship to Shug that Celie comes to accept herself as someone worthy of being loved. And I think what is so crucial in *The Color Purple* is that she goes on through that relationship to have a powerful and loving bond with Albert. So Walker does not pose lesbianism as an anti-male alternative, but instead says that when a person becomes more self-loving they are more able to love, understand, and forgive others. So that at the end of this novel we can see Celie and Albert, both of whom have grown in their capacity to be more self-loving, say to one another, we are truly companions of the spirit now. It touched me when Albert says to Celie, "We're just two old fools under the stars." They can come back in some kind of harmony with one another precisely because they have undergone a conversion. Celie's same-sex love relation allows them to love themselves more fully.

CW I can see that, but I think one of the dangers in both of those options (lesbianism and interaction with men who are not of African descent) is to think that somehow relations of domination will not be reproduced within those relationships as well. To think that somehow just moving from the Black man to the White man will provide a less abusive context is flawed. Even with lesbian relationships, to think they are somehow free from domination, racism, internalized sexism, tension, anxiety, and possibly abuse is naive. The tensions in these alternative relationships won't necessarily manifest themselves in the same way, but they won't disappear either.

bh But are Black women choosing away from Black men because so few Black men are willing to stand up and tell you that their lives are committed to the principles of feminism?

CW Why do you have to have a mate who subscribes to your own principles? Why couldn't you have a mate who said, I am committed to loving this person who is committed to the principles of feminism?

When I think about my own primary relationship, I do not ask that my wife also be committed to my Democratic Socialist practices.

bh But I think it is totally different because she, as an individual, is not a capitalist who oppresses you. Whereas if we conceptualize patriarchy as a system of domination that actually is most reenacted in the domestic sphere, then whether or not a person is actually committed to feminism informs how we can live as two heterosexuals together.

I have loved and been partnered with men, who don't see themselves as religious, even though religion is an integral part of my daily life, and they haven't actively oppressed me for being religious. But being with a man who was not committed to feminism might mean that I was with someone who was actually operating against me or undermining my feminist commitment.

CW But there is a middle ground. I can envision a man that, because he loved you would never oppress you, though he would not necessarily subscribe to the principles of feminism.

bh Whereas I would say that any man who would not oppress a woman within patriarchy is already subscribing to the principles for feminism.

CW Yes, I see.

bh He doesn't have to take on the language but he is already a transformed man within the constructs of patriarchy. Because patriarchy is always willing to reward him for the subjugation of women. It would also not be satisfactory to me to be with a man who, albeit did not want to subordinate me, treated other women with contempt.

Particularly when you are a well known Black woman, you run into categories of men who think that you are somehow different and you are more worthy of respect and adoration than other women, and that is not acceptable to me politically or personally. To raise a woman up, even as you would go out in daily life and be an agent of exploitation and oppression of other women, is an insidious thing.

CW It's a tough issue because it seems to me every man, including myself, is thoroughly shaped by patriarchal values which means that our values, no matter how feminist we proclaim ourselves to be, are inevitably tainted all the way through.

bh But that's why I said a commitment.

As we talk more about transformative possibilities for Black men and women we need to explore more than just romantic relationships; we need to talk seriously about friendship. It has been a really healing thing for me to recognize that we are wounded. We are wounded in so many areas that what I think is magical and wonderful is when I meet another Black person who says they are about the business of attending to their wounds. Which means they don't have to be perfect, they don't have to have wiped out every trace of sexism, homophobia, classism, and internalized racism. Rather it is the commitment to the process of change and convergence which opens up the possibility of love, renewal, and reconciliation.

CW But it has got to be a commitment that has some concrete manifestations. For so many people, liberatory consciousness is not just fashionable, it is profitable for their careers.

bh I think a great deal about the nature of process. I work here at Oberlin College with Calvin Hernton. If we look at Hernton's earlier books such as *Sex and Racism in America*, we see how profoundly negative and sexist they were in the way they talked about Black women. Then the Hernton of a few years later—and I truly believe he had a conversion experience along the way—begins to critique his own misogyny and the misogyny of other Black men. He writes an essay like "Black Women Writers and the Sexual Mountain," and he gets dogged out by Black women and Black men alike who see him as an opportunist. Now, I sit back and say to myself, is it not dangerous for us to immediately want to label this person opportunist when what he is saying is really trying to subvert the patriarchal norm, trying to create a space of intervention? I am less invested in judging him as opportunistic than I am in accepting the potential positiveness of that intervention. I think it is a dangerous thing to want men to change but then perceive a man as changing too rapidly or getting some perks from making the change and denigrate that transformation. I think we have to be very careful about that, otherwise we make it seem like it is a no-win situation for Black men, a no-win situation for

men in general. At the same time, you are absolutely right to demand concrete manifestations.

I look at our friendship over the years and there were times
when I thought you were not doing all you could to combat sexism. Then I look at the areas where I have seen you grow in your
thought and action. Take, for example, our interview that appeared
in *Emerge*. One of the things that disturbed us mutually was the
knowledge that Black women readers of *Emerge* are frequently
alienated by the magazine because of its sometimes exclusively
Black male perspective. Now I'm not sure the Cornel West I met
years ago would have acknowledged that, by *my* interviewing
you, I was being positioned as the subordinate voice in the interview. The first thing you said when the *Emerge* representative arrived was that this really should be a dialogue, because we are
equals in the enterprise of Black intellectuality. Not only was that
an act of feminist solidarity but a concrete manifestation of your
commitment to Black feminist principles.

CW I grew up in traditional Black patriarchal culture and
there is no doubt that I'm going to take a great many unconscious,
but present, patriarchal complicities to the grave because it is so
deeply ensconced in how I look at the world. Therefore, very
much like alcoholism, drug addiction, or racism, patriarchy is a disease and we are in perennial recovery and relapse. So you have to
get up every morning and struggle against it.

bh That reminds me once again of the Donohue show with
Shahrazad Ali, and the brutal way in which she called Haki
Madhabuti a wimp. And there he was: gentle, respectful, not rude
or silencing. Black women alongside Black men must begin to reconceptualize what we think of as masculine if we want to see
some kind of gender revolution in Black community and in Black
relationships. Madhabuti was the embodiment of a Black man
showing respect to a Black woman. And her abuse of that respect
by actually trying to suggest that he is not a real man revealed the
full horror of a male-identified woman. I have to admit that sometimes in my classes, young brothers, engaged in feminist thinking,
come to me and say, my girlfriend wants me to be more dominant
because that's what she thinks a man is.

One of the ways I feel we suffered the loss of Malcolm X is
that many people do not realize, having only seen his participation
in public life where he was a very forceful man, that in his private
life his children have spoken about what a caring, gentle, nurturing
presence he was. We need a sense that there is no monolithic con-

struction of masculinity, that the whole person is capable of being strong at those moments of life which require a certain assertion of agency and strength but then also to be capable of generosity and quietude and nurturance in other arenas. This is the crucial work in gender relations which has not been done for us as Black people: to come up with models of Black masculinity that differ from a macho norm. And we as Black women must also undergo a conversion experience so that we can appreciate and affirm those Black men. Because it is true that part of American sexual mythology is "good guys finish last." So why should a brother try to treat sisters right if he sees them passing him up for Mr. no good?

CW Mr. Superfly.

bh Women buy into the mystique of macho behavior and create a fantasy man who is macho and aggressive yet does not wield that machismo violently against them. This attempted denial of the brutality inherent to the machismo character is dangerous to the lives and psyches of Black women. Because Black women collectively have not begun to fully critique conventional notions of femininity, we are still dependent on affirming our constructed femininity with its alleged counterpart, machismo. Only when we begin to critique these notions more fully and transform ourselves accordingly can we be fully open to radical Black men rethinking masculinity.

CW It must have to do with a Black fear of intimacy. The intimate presupposes vulnerability.

So many Black women who, when allowing themselves to be vulnerable, have been crushed, so that they give up on genuine intimacy and invest instead in superficial forms of status and superficial notions of beauty.

Oftentimes what Black women mean when they talk about a strong man is not domination in the negative sense but someone secure, reliable, and trustworthy. The metaphor has more to do with a rock than a whip. Now there is nothing wrong with a rock, everybody needs a rock. Black women especially have had less access to rocks, less access to security, reliability, and trustworthiness. Therefore the interpretation of Black women's need to have something to fall back on in times of need, despair, and grief, and their consequent desire for men to be dominant can be recast in much healthier terms.

bh Coming out of a dysfunctional family setting, I have had to learn to trust myself to provide certain kinds of care for myself, and in trusting that I can provide those kinds of care, I can be more trusting of another person's capacity to provide that care. If I experience myself as always "losing it" in times of crisis then I need an exaggerated expression from you that you can sustain me in times of crisis. So to the extent that I develop my own inner capacity for self-care, to the extent that I can be a solid rock for myself, I can also be a solid rock for you, and simultaneously I won't need you to prove that to me all the time.

Many Black men feel they have been driven into the grave by heart attacks and strokes while trying to appear as that solid rock for the individuals in their lives—be they children, spouse, lover, gay companion, what have you, who don't ever want to see them break down. These individuals don't want to see the person they labeled "provider" as having times of vulnerability. Which reaffirms why critiques of conventional notions of patriarchy are so important. Because that model of manhood denies the full humanity of men, denies that there are moments in men's lives when they need to say, "I can't go out there and do this stressful thing that is breaking my spirit anymore." Black men have not felt, especially the many Black men who have been strong providers, who have carried the mantle of representing a strong, dignified Black manhood, that they need a space to articulate their emotionaly vulnerability.

CW Yes, there can be no intimacy without mutual vulnerability.

What I also meant by "rock" is...

bh Constancy. That there can be no real intimacy without commitment, and commitment is formed in relations of constancy. I think about you and me as friends and how we have nurtured our friendship through time. If we saw each other only once a year what would happen to our level of trust, how would we create a history together that could hold and sustain the difficult times in our lives and in our friendship? Not that I believe distance necessarily inhibits intimacy, but intimacy requires cultivation, and cultivation requires commitment and constancy.

CW So now we see our community grappling on a large scale with a shared sense of mutual betrayal. Since integration, we have not cultivated enough committed relationships to ourselves, our community, and by extension people of African descent. This internal cultivation of love and support enables us to interact with non-African peoples in a more humane manner.

bh How do you think this relates to questions of sexual fidelity and commitment? Certainly one of the major problems in the Black community is AIDS education and prevention. Black people tend to deny the reality of homosexuality, bisexuality, or promiscuity in any orientation. Consequently our sexual stigmas don't allow us to take appropriate measures to begin serious prevention and treatment campaigns within the community. If we are going to talk about, as Ali does, non-monogamous relationships, we have got to also be talking about a more public discourse on sexuality, as a matter of self-preservation. I don't say this exclusively about AIDS but also about the many STDs we know are so rampant in this society as a whole right now.

One of the major issues facing us as a people is the struggle to create a fulfilling sexuality that is linked to relations of commitment and care. Unlike the dominant White culture, Black people have come out of African diasporic conditions where sexual pleasure may not be viewed as taking place in the same location as emotional fulfillment. Clearly, if we look at the divorce rates of heterosexual Black people, the coupling practices of Black gays and lesbians, there is much that would indicate that we need to re-vision the place of sexuality in love relationships—we need to critique sport fucking. Across our various sexual preferences and practices, issues of power and desire are played out in the arena of sexual seduction and conquest. A Black man who feels impotent in most of the arenas of his life, work, and self-image may feel like the only place where he can overcome that sense of impotency, and experience himself as dominating power person is a sexual playing field where he manipulates and plays partners off against one another, or where he drives one woman crazy through deceit and lying. By critiquing sport fucking and power playing that is ultimately destructive and dehumanizing, I don't mean to suggest that all forms of non-monogamy are absolutely negative.

I have not been a person who has ever felt that monogamy was the be all and end all. As M. Scott Peck says in his popular book *The Road Less Traveled*, you can love more than one person if you are capable of it. That means that you have to have the time and the space and the generosity of heart, and most of us do not have that. Most of us cannot function so that we truly have love relations.

CW So many people can hardly love one person.

bh Absolutely.

CW Or love themselves.

bh And these are the issues facing us when we have popular movements that are pushing polygamy in Black community life. That the conditions of who we are, the way we are emotionally ravaged daily makes it hard for us to say that we can love more than one person. We can certainly have sex with more than one person. And we have got to make a distinction.

CW You can't take a man who talks about polygamy seriously unless he tells you it applies to women as well. Because sexuality is so much a part of the exercise of power in a patriarchal society, you are going to see that double standard always in play on the level of practice.

bh Cornel, I am very interested in the relationship between Black people's capacity to love one another and our notions of spirituality. One of the disturbing things I see is many Black people who are no longer engaged with Black religious experience. This has been very damaging to our collective psyches because one of the major arenas of our lives in which we had a sense of hope came from Black religious experience. The sense that no matter how downtrodden you are, no matter how beaten down you are, there remains the possibility of redemption and salvation. That message of hope was an integral survival force in Black life. So how can we talk about revitalized notions of spirituality in Black life? Is that possible?

CW Yes, I think it is possible and I think it is important to understand spirituality here as that which sustains hope. One way of talking about this is to say the only hope that Black people have is that Black people with hope never lose hope. In the past it has certainly been true that Christianity was the major conduit for hope. Yet I don't think Christianity has necessarily had a monopoly on hope in the Black community because there are secular forms, other religious forms, Islamic forms, Judaic forms, and Buddhist forms in the Black community. But in our present day situation, in which hopelessness is becoming more and more pervasive, it seems to me that we have got to revitalize not just Christian but all conduits of hope. As a Christian, I speak from the Christian condition, but what I have to say ought to have relevance for all the different religious traditions. What then becomes so difficult is that the nihilism running rampant in our communities cuts hope off. One of the worst things that could happen to the Black community is that those whose work invokes hope end up being religious hustlers and charlatans, thereby destroying trust. That is one of the predicaments we find ourselves in today: that people—especially leaders—who talk about hope tend to be manipulative.

8

The Dilemma of the Black Intellectual *
by Cornel West

The peculiarities of the American social structure, and the position of the intellectual class within it, make the functional role of the negro intellectual a special one. The negro intellectual must deal intimately with the White power structure and cultural apparatus, and the inner realities of the Black world at one and the same time. But in order to function successfully in this role, he has to be acutely aware of the nature of the American social dynamic and how it monitors the ingredients of class stratifications in American society....Therefore the functional role of the negro intellectual demands that he *cannot* be absolutely separated from either the Black or White world.

—Harold Cruse
The Crisis of the Negro Intellectual (1967)

The contemporary Black intellectual faces a grim predicament. Caught between an insolent American society and insouciant Black community, the Afro-American who takes seriously the life of the mind inhabits an isolated and insulated world. This condition has little to do with the motives and intentions of Black intellectuals; rather it is an objective situation created by circumstances

---

* This article first appeared in *Cultural Critique,* Volume 1, Number 1, 1985.

not of their own choosing. In this meditative essay, I will explore this dilemma of the Black intellectual and suggest various ways of understanding and transforming it.

On Becoming a Black Intellectual

The choice of becoming a Black intellectual is an act of self-imposed marginality; it assures a peripheral status in and to the Black community. The quest for literacy indeed is a fundamental theme in Afro-American history and a basic impulse in the Black community. But for Blacks, as with most Americans, the uses for literacy are usually perceived to be for more substantive pecuniary benefits than those of the writer, artist, teacher, or professor. The reasons some Black people choose to become serious intellectuals are diverse. But in most cases these reasons can be traced back to a common root: a conversion-like experience with a highly influential teacher or peer that convinced one to dedicate one's life to the activities of reading, writing, and conversing for the purposes of individual pleasure, personal worth, and political enhancement of Black (and often other oppressed) people.

The way in which one becomes a Black intellectual is highly problematic. This is so because the traditional roads others travel to become intellectuals in American society have only recently been opened—and remain quite difficult. The main avenues are the academy or the literate subcultures of art, culture, and politics. Prior to the acceptance of Black undergraduate students to elite White universities and colleges in the late Sixties, select Black educational institutions served as the initial stimulus for potential Black intellectuals. And in all honesty, there were relatively more and better Black intellectuals then than now. After a decent grounding in a Black college, where self-worth and self-confidence were affirmed, bright Black students then matriculated to leading White institutions to be trained by liberal sympathetic scholars often of renowned stature. Stellar figures such as W.E.B. DuBois, E. Franklin Frazier, and John Hope Franklin were products of this system. For those Black intellectuals-to-be who missed college opportunities for financial or personal reasons, there were literate subcultures—especially in the large urban centers—of writers, painters, musicians, and politicos for unconventional educational enhancement. Major personages such as Richard Wright, Ralph Ellison, and James Baldwin were products of this process.

Ironically, the present day academy and contemporary literate subcultures present more obstacles for young Black intellectuals than those in decades past. This is so for three basic reasons. First, the attitudes of White scholars in the academy are quite different than those in the past. It is much more difficult for Black students, especially graduate students, to be taken seriously as *potential scholars and intellectuals,* owing to the managerial ethos of our universities and colleges (in which less time is spent with students) and to the vulgar (racist!) perceptions fueled by affirmative action programs which pollute many Black student-White professor relations.

Second, literate subcultures are less open to Blacks now than they were three or four decades ago, not because White avant-garde journals or leftist groups are more racist today but rather because heated political and cultural issues, such as the legacy of the Black Power movement, the Israeli/Palestinian conflict, the invisibility of Africa in American political discourse, have created rigid lines of demarcation and distance between Black and White intellectuals. Needless to say, Black presence in leading liberal journals like *The New York Review of Books* and *The New York Times Book Review* is negligible—nearly non-existent. And more leftist periodicals such as *Dissent, Socialist Review, The Nation,* and *Telos,* or avant-garde scholarly ones like *Diacritics, Salmagundi, Partisan Review,* and *Raritan* do not do much better. Only *Monthly Review, The Massachusetts Review, Boundary 2,* and *Social Text* make persistent efforts to cover Black subject-matter and have regular Black contributors. The point here is not mere finger-pointing at negligent journals (though it would not hurt matters!), but rather an attempt to highlight the racially separatist publishing patterns and practices of American intellectual life which are characteristic of the chasm between Black and White intellectuals.

Third, the general politicization of American intellectual life (in the academy and outside), along with the rightward ideological drift, constitutes a hostile climate for the making of Black intellectuals. To some extent, this has always been so, but the ideological capitulation of the significant segment of former left-liberals to the new-style conservatism and old-style imperialism has left Black students and Black professors with few allies in the academy and in influential periodicals. This hostile climate requires that Black intellectuals fall back upon their own resources—institutions, journals, and periodicals—which, in turn, reinforces the de facto racially separatist practices of American intellectual life.

The tragedy of Black intellectual activity is that the Black institutional support for such activity is in shambles. The quantity and quality of Black intellectual exchange is at its worst since the Civil War. There is no major Black academic journal; no major Black intellectual magazine; no major Black periodical of highbrow journalism; not even a major Black newspaper of national scope. In short, the Black infrastructure for intellectual discourse and dialogue is nearly non-existent. This tragedy is, in part, the price for integration—which has yielded mere marginal Black groups within the professional disciplines of a fragmented academic community. But this tragedy also has to do with the refusal of Black intellectuals to establish and sustain their own institutional mechanisms of criticism and self-criticism, organized in such a way that people of whatever color would be able to contribute to it. This refusal over the past decade is significant in that it has lessened the appetite for, and the capacity to withstand, razor-sharp criticism among many Black intellectuals whose formative years were passed in a kind of intellectual vacuum. So, besides the external hostile climate, the tradition of serious Black intellectual activity is also threatened from within.

The creation of an intelligentsia is a monumental task. Yet Black churches and colleges, along with significant White support, served as resources for the first Black intellectuals with formal training. The formation of high-quality habits of criticism and international networks of serious intellectual exchange among a relatively isolated and insulated intelligentsia is a gargantuan endeavor. Yet Black intellectuals have little choice: either continued intellectual lethargy on the edges of the academy and literate subcultures unnoticed by the Black community, or insurgent creative activity on the margins of the mainstream ensconced within bludgeoning new infrastructures.

Black Intellectuals and the Black Community

The paucity of Black infrastructures for intellectual activity results, in part, from the inability of Black intellectuals to gain respect and support from the Black community—and especially the Black middle class. In addition to the general anti-intellectual tenor of American society, there is a deep distrust and suspicion of the Black community toward Black intellectuals. This distrust and suspicion stem not simply from the usual arrogant and haughty disposition of intellectuals toward ordinary folk, but, more importantly, from the widespread refusal of Black intellectuals to remain, in some visible way, organically linked with Afro-American cultural life. The relatively high rates of exogamous marriage, the abandonment of Black institutions, and the preoccupations with Euro-American intellectual products are often perceived by the Black community as intentional efforts to escape the negative stigma of Blackness or viewed as symptoms of self-hatred. And the minimal immediate impact of Black intellectual activity on the Black community and American society reinforces common perceptions of the impotence, even uselessness, of Black intellectuals. In good American fashion, the Black community lauds those Black intellectuals who excel as *political activists* and *cultural artists;* the life of the mind is viewed as neither possessing intrinsic virtues nor harboring emancipatory possibilities—solely short-term political gain and social status.

This truncated perception of intellectual activity is widely held by Black intellectuals themselves. Given the constraints upon Black upward social mobility and the pressures for status and affluence among middle-class peers, many Black intellectuals principally seek material gain and cultural prestige. Since these intellectuals are members of an anxiety-ridden and status-hungry Black middle class, their proclivities are understandable and, to some extent, justifiable, since most intellectuals are in search of recognition, status, power, and often wealth. For Black intellectuals this search requires immersing oneself in and addressing oneself to the very culture and society which degrade and devalue the Black community from whence one comes. And, to put it crudely, most Black intellectuals tend to fall within the two camps created by this predicament: "successful" ones, distant from (and usually condescending toward) the Black community, and "unsuccessful" ones, disdainful of the White intellectual world. But both camps remain marginal to the Black community—dangling between two worlds with little or no Black infrastructural base. Therefore, the "successful" Black intellectual capitulates, often uncritically, to the prevailing paradigms and research programs of the White bourgeois academy, and the "unsuccessful" Black intellectual remains encapsulated within the parochial discourses of Afro-American intellectual life. The alternatives of meretricious pseudo-cosmopolitanism and tendentious, cathartic provincialism loom large in the lives of Black intellectuals. And the Black community views both alternatives with distrust and disdain—and with good reason. Neither alternative has had a positive impact on the Black community. The major Black intellectuals from W.E.B. DuBois and St. Clair Drake to Ralph Ellison and Toni Morrison have shunned both alternatives.

This situation has resulted in the major obstacle confronting Black intellectuals: the inability to transmit and sustain the requisite institutional mechanisms for the persistence of a discernible intellectual tradition. The racism of American society, the relative lack of Black community support, and hence the dangling status of Black intellectuals, have prevented the creation of a rich heritage of intellectual exchange, intercourse, and dialogue. There indeed have been grand Black intellectual achievements, but such achievements do not substitute for tradition.

I would suggest that there are two *organic* intellectual traditions in Afro-American life: *the Black Christian tradition of preaching* and *the Black musical tradition of performance*. Both traditions, though undoubtedly linked to the life of the mind, are oral, improvisational, and histrionic. Both traditions are rooted in Black life and possess precisely what the literate forms of Black intellectual activity lack: institutional matrices over time and space within which there are accepted rules of procedure, criteria for judgment, canons for assessing performance, models of past achievement and present emulation, and an acknowledged succession and accumulation of superb accomplishments. The richness, diversity, and vitality of the traditions of Black preaching and Black music stand in strong contrast to the paucity, even poverty, of Black literate intellectual production. There simply have been no Black literate intellectuals who have mastered their craft commensurate with the achievements of Louis Armstrong, Charlie Parker, or Rev. Manuel Scott—just as there are no Black literate intellectuals today comparable to Miles Davis, Sarah Vaughan, or Rev. Gardner Taylor. This is so not because there have been or are no first-rate, Black, literate intellectuals, but rather because without strong institutional channels to sustain traditions, great achievement is impossible. And, to be honest, Black America has yet to produce a great, literate intellectual, with the sole exception of Toni Morrison. There indeed have been superb ones—DuBois, Frazier, Ellison, Baldwin, Hurston—and many good ones. But none can compare to the heights achieved by Black preachers and, especially musicians.

What is most troubling about Black literate intellectual activity is that, as it slowly evolved out of the Black Christian tradition and interacted more intimately with secular Euro-American styles and forms, it seemed as if, by the latter part of the 20th century, maturation would set it. Yet, as we approach the last few years of this century, Black literate intellectual activity has declined in both quantity and quality. As I noted earlier, this is so primarily because of relatively greater Black integration into postindustrial capitalist America with its bureaucratized, elite universities, dull middlebrow colleges, and decaying high schools, which have little concern for and confidence in Black students as potential intellectuals. Needless to say, the predicament of the Black intellectual is inseparable from that of the Black community—especially the Black middle-class community—in American society. And only a fundamental transformation of American society can possibly change the situation of the Black community and the Black intellectual. And though my own Christian skepticism regarding human totalistic schemes for change chasten my deep socialist sentiments regarding radically democratic and libertarian socio-economic and cultural arrangements, I shall forego these larger issues and focus on more specific ways to enhance the quantity and quality of Black literate intellectual activity in the United States. This focus shall take the form of sketching four models for Black intellectual activity, with the intent to promote the crystallization of infrastructures for such activity.

The Bourgeois Model: Black Intellectual as Humanist

For Black intellectuals, the bourgeois model of intellectual activity is problematic. On the one hand, the racist heritage—aspects of the exclusionary and repressive effects of White academic institutions and humanistic scholarship—puts Black intellectuals on the defensive: there is always the need to assert and defend the humanity of Black people, including their ability and capacity to reason logically, think coherently, and write lucidly. The weight of this inescapable burden for Black students in the White academy has often determined the content and character of Black intellectual activity. In fact, Black intellectual life remains largely preoccupied with such defensiveness, with "successful" Black intellectuals often proud of their White approval and "unsuccessful" ones usually scornful of their White rejection. This concern is especially acute among the first generation of Black intellectuals accepted as teachers and scholars within elite White universities and colleges, largely a post-1968 phenomenon. Only with the publication of the intimate memoirs of these Black intellectuals and their students will we have the gripping stories of how this defensiveness cut at much of the heart of their intellectual activity and creativity within White academic contexts. Yet, however personally painful such battles have been, they had to be fought, given the racist milieu of American intellectual and academic life. These battles will continue but with much less negative consequences for the younger generation because of the struggles by the older Black trailblazers.

On the other hand, the state of siege raging in the Black community requires that Black intellectuals accent the practical dimension of their work. And the prestige and status, as well as the skills and techniques provided by the White bourgeois academy, render it attractive for the task at hand. The accentuation of the practical dimension holds for most Black intellectuals, regardless of ideological persuasion—even more than for the stereotypical, pragmatic American intellectual. This is so not simply because of the power-seeking lifestyles and status-oriented dispositions of many Black intellectuals, but also because of their relatively small number, which forces them to play multiple roles vis-à-vis the Black community and, in addition, intensifies their need for self-vindication— the attempt to justify to themselves that, given such unique opportunities and privileges, they are spending their time as they ought—which often results in activistic and pragmatic interests.

The linchpin of the bourgeois model is academic legitimation and placement. Without the proper certificate, degree, and position, the bourgeois model loses its *raison d'etre*. The influence and attractiveness of the bourgeois model permeate the American academic system; yet the effectiveness of the bourgeois model is credible for Black intellectuals only if they possess sufficient legitimacy and placement. Such legitimacy and placement will give one access to select networks and contacts which may facilitate Black impact on public policies. This seems to have been the aim of the first generation of Blacks trained in elite White institutions (though not permitted to teach there), given their predominant interests in the social sciences.

The basic problem with the bourgeois model is that it is existentially and intellectually stultifying for Black intellectuals. It is existentially debilitating because it not only generates anxieties of defensiveness on the part of Black intellectuals; it also thrives on them. The need for hierarchical ranking and the deep-seated racism shot through bourgeois humanistic scholarship cannot provide Black intellectuals with either the proper ethos or conceptual framework to overcome a defensive posture. And charges of intellectual inferiority can never be met upon the opponent's terrain—to try to do so only intensifies one's anxieties. Rather the terrain itself must be viewed as part and parcel of an antiquated form of life unworthy of setting the terms of contemporary discourse.

The bourgeois model sets intellectual limits, in that one is prone to adopt uncritically prevailing paradigms predominant in the bourgeois academy because of the pressures of practical tasks and deferential emulation. Every intellectual passes through some kind of apprenticeship stage in which s/he learns the language and style of the authorities, but when s/he is already viewed as marginally talented s/he may be either excessively encouraged or misleadingly discouraged to critically examine paradigms deemed marginal by the authorities. This hostile environment results in the suppression of one's critical analyses and in the limited use of one's skills in a manner considered legitimate and practical.

Despite its limitations, the bourgeois model is inescapable for most Black intellectuals. This is so because most of the important and illuminating discourses in the country take place in White bourgeois academic institutions and because the more significant intellectuals teach in such places. Many of the elite White universities and colleges remain high-powered schools of education, learning, and training principally due to large resources and civil traditions that provide the leisure time and atmosphere necessary for sustained and serious intellectual endeavor. So, aside from the few serious autodidactic Black intellectuals (who often have impressive scope but lack grounding and depth), Black intellectuals must pass through the White bourgeois academy (or its Black imitators).

Black academic legitimation and placement can provide a foothold in American intellectual life so that Black infrastructures for intellectual activity can be created. At present, there is a small yet significant Black presence within the White bourgeois academic organizations, and it is able to produce newsletters and small periodicals. The next step is to more broadly institutionalize Black intellectual presence, as the Society of Black Philosophers of New York has done, by publishing journals anchored in a discipline (crucial for the careers of prospective professors) yet relevant to other disciplines. It should be noted that such a Black infrastructure for intellectual activity should attract persons of whatever hue or color. Black literary critics and especially Black psychologists are far ahead of other Black intellectuals in this regard with journals such as *The Black American Literature Forum, The College Lan-guage Association,* and *The Journal of Black Psychology.*

Black academic legitimation and placement also can result in Black control over a portion of, or significant participation within, the larger White infrastructures for intellectual activity. This has not yet occurred on a broad scale. More Black representation is needed on the editorial boards of significant journals so that more Black intellectual presence is permitted. This process is much slower and has less visibility, yet, given the hegemony of the bourgeois model, it must be pursued by those so inclined.

The bourgeois model is, in some fundamental and ultimate sense, more part of the problem than the "solution" in regard to Black intellectuals. Yet, since we live our lives daily and penultimately within this system, those of us highly critical of the bourgeois model must try to transform it, in part from within the White bourgeois academy. For Black intellectuals—in alliance with non-Black progressive intellectuals—this means creating and augmenting infrastructures for Black intellectual activity.

The Marxist Model: Black Intellectual as Revolutionary

Among many Black intellectuals, there is a knee-jerk reaction to the severe limitations of the bourgeois model (and capitalist society)—namely, to adopt the Marxist model. This adoption satisfies certain basic needs of the Black intelligentsia: the need for social relevance, political engagement, and organizational involvement. The Marxist model also provides entry into the least xenophobic White intellectual subculture available to Black intellectuals.

The Marxist model privileges the activity of Black intellectuals and promotes their prophetic role. As Harold Cruse has noted, such privileging is highly circumscribed and rarely accents the theoretical dimension of Black intellectual activity. In short, the Marxist privileging of Black intellectuals often reeks of condescension that confines Black prophetic roles to spokespersons and organizers; only rarely are they allowed to function as creative thinkers who warrant serious critical attention. It is no accident that the relatively large numbers of Black intellectuals attracted to Marxism over the past sixty years have yet to produce a major Black Marxist theoretician. Only W.E.B. DuBois's *Black Reconstruction* (1935), Oliver Cox's *Caste, Class and Race* (1948), and, to some degree,

Harold Cruse's *The Crisis of the Negro Intellectual* (1967) are even candidates for such a designation. This is so, not because of the absence of Black intellectual talent in the Marxist camp, but rather because of the absence of the kind of tradition and community (including intense critical exchange) that would allow such talent to flower.

In stark contrast to the bourgeois model, the Marxist model neither generates Black-intellectual defensiveness nor provides an adequate analytical apparatus for short-term public policies. Rather the Marxist model yields Black-intellectual self-satisfaction which often inhibits growth; it also highlights social structural constraints with little practical direction regarding conjunctural opportunities. This self-satisfaction results in either dogmatic submission to and upward mobility within sectarian party or pre-party formations, or marginal placement in the bourgeois academy equipped with cantankerous Marxist rhetoric and sometimes insightful analysis utterly divorced from the integral dynamics, concrete realities, and progressive possibilities of the Black community. The preoccupation with social structural constraints tends to produce either preposterous, chiliastic projections or paralyzing, pessimistic pronouncements. Both such projections and pronouncements have as much to do with the self-image of Black Marxist intellectuals as with the prognosis for Black liberation.

It is often claimed that "Marxism is the false consciousness of the radicalized, bourgeois intelligentsia." For Black intellectuals, the Marxist model functions in a more complex manner than this glib formulation permits. On the one hand, the Marxist model is liberating for Black intellectuals, in that it promotes critical consciousness and attitudes toward the dominant bourgeois paradigms and research programs. Marxism provides attractive roles for Black intellectuals—usually highly visible leadership roles—and infuses new meaning and urgency into their work. On the other hand, the Marxist model is debilitating for Black intellectuals because the cathartic needs it satisfies tend to stifle the further development of Black critical consciousness and attitudes.

The Marxist model, despite its shortcomings, is more part of the "solution" than part of the problem for Black intellectuals. This is so because Marxism is the brook of fire—the purgatory—of our postmodern times. Black intellectuals must pass through it, come to terms with it, and creatively respond to it if Black intellectual activity is to reach any recognizable level of sophistication and refinement.

The Foucaultian Model: Black Intellectual as Postmodern Skeptic

As Western intellectual life moves more deeply into crisis, and as Black intellectuals become more fully integrated into intellectual life—or into "the culture of careful and critical discourse" (as the late Alvin Gouldner called it)—a new model appears on the horizon. This model, based primarily upon the influential work of the late Michel Foucault, unequivocally rejects the bourgeois model and eschews the Marxist model. It constitutes one of the most exciting intellectual challenges of our day: the Foucaultian project of historical nominalism. This detailed investigation into the complex relations of knowledge and power, discourses and politics, cognition and social control compels intellectuals to rethink and redefine their self-image and function in our contemporary situation.

The Foucaultian model and project are attractive to Black intellectuals primarily because they speak to the Black postmodern predicament, defined by the rampant xenophobia of bourgeois humanism predominant in the whole academy, the waning attraction to orthodox reductionist and scientific versions of Marxism, and the need for reconceptualization regarding the specificity and complexity of Afro-American oppression. Foucault's deep anti-bourgeois sentiments, explicit post-Marxist convictions, and profound preoccupations with those viewed as radically "other" by dominant discourses and traditions are quite seductive for politicized Black intellectuals wary of antiquated panaceas for Black liberation.

Foucault's specific analyses of the "political economy of truth"—the study of the discursive ways in which and institutional means by which "regimes of truth" are constituted by societies over space and time—result in a new conception of the intellectual. This conception no longer rests upon the smooth transmittance of "the best that has been thought and said," as in the bourgeois humanist model, nor on the utopian energies of the Marxist model. Rather the postmodern situation requires "the specific intellectual" who shuns the labels of scientificity, civility, and prophecy, and instead delves into the specificity of the political, economic, and cultural matrices within which regimes of truth are produced, distributed, circulated, and consumed. No longer should intellectuals deceive themselves by believing—as do humanist and Marxist intellectuals—that they are struggling "on behalf" of the truth; rather the problem is the struggle over the very status of truth and the vast institutional mechanisms which account for this status. The favored code words of "science," "taste," "tact," "ideology," "progress," and "liberation" of bourgeois humanism and Marxism are no longer applicable to the self-image of postmodern intellectuals. Instead, the new key terms become those of "regime of truth," "power/knowledge," and "discursive practices."

Foucault's notion of the specific intellectual rests upon his demystification of conservative, liberal, and Marxist rhetoric which restore, resituate, and reconstruct intellectuals' self-identities so that they remain captive to and supportive of institutional forms of domination and control. These rhetorics authorize and legitimate, in different ways, the privileged status of intellectuals, which not only reproduce ideological divisions between intellectual and manual labor but also reinforce disciplinary mechanisms of subjection and subjugation. This self-authorizing is best exemplified in the claims made by intellectuals that they "safeguard" the achievements of highbrow culture or "represent" the "universal interests" of particular classes and groups. In Afro-American intellectual history, similar self-authorizing claims such as "the talented tenth," "prophets in the wilderness," "articulators of a Black aesthetic," "creators of a Black renaissance," and "vanguard of a revolutionary movement" are widespread.

The Foucaultian model promotes a leftist form of postmodern skepticism; that is, it encourages an intense and incessant interrogation of power-laden discourses in the service of neither restoration, reformation, nor revolution, but rather of revolt. And the kind of revolt enacted by intellectuals consists of the disrupting and dismantling of prevailing "regimes of truth" —including their repressive effects—of present day societies. This model suits the critical, skeptical, and historical concerns of progressive Black intellectuals and provides a sophisticated excuse for ideological and social distance from insurgent Black movements for liberation. By conceiving of intellectual work as oppositional political praxis, it satisfies the leftist self-image of Black intellectuals, and, by making a fetish of critical consciousness, it encapsulates Black intellectual activity within the comfortable bourgeois academy of postmodern America.

The Insurgency Model: Black Intellectual as Critical, Organic Catalyst

Black intellectuals can learn much from each of the three previous models, yet should not uncritically adopt any one of them.

This is so because the bourgeois, Marxist, and Foucaultian models indeed relate to, but do not adequately speak to, the uniqueness of the Black intellectual predicament. This uniqueness remains relatively unexplored, and will remain so until Black intellectuals articulate a new "regime of truth" linked to, yet not confined by, indigenous institutional practices permeated by the kinetic orality and emotional physicality, the rhythmic syncopation, the protean improvisation, and the religious, rhetorical, and antiphonal elements of Afro-American life. Such articulation depends, in part, upon elaborate Black infrastructures which put a premium on creative and cultivated Black thought; it also entails intimate knowledge of prevailing Euro-American "regimes of truth" which must be demystified, deconstructed, and decomposed in ways which enhance and enrich future Black intellectual life. The new "regime of truth" to be pioneered by Black thinkers is neither a hermetic discourse (or set of discourses), which safeguards mediocre Black intellectual production, nor the latest fashion of Black writing, which is often motivated by the desire to parade for the White bourgeois intellectual establishment. Rather it is inseparable from the emergence of new cultural forms which prefigure (and point toward) a post- (not anti-) Western civilization. At present, such talk may seem mere dream and fantasy. So we shall confine ourselves to the first step: Black insurgency and the role of the Black intellectual.

The major priority of Black intellectuals should be the creation or reactivation of institutional networks that promote high-quality critical habits primarily for the purpose of Black insurgency. An intelligentsia without institutionalized critical consciousness is blind, and critical consciousness severed from collective insurgency is empty. The central task of postmodern Black intellectuals is to stimulate, hasten, and enable alternative perceptions and practices by dislodging prevailing discourses and powers. This can be done only by intense intellectual work and engaged insurgent praxis.

The insurgency model for Black intellectual activity builds upon, yet goes beyond, the previous three models. From the bourgeois model, it recuperates the emphasis on human will and heroic effort. Yet the insurgency model refuses to conceive of this will and effort in individualistic and elitist terms. Instead of the solitary hero, embattled exile, and isolated genius—the intellectual as star, celebrity, commodity—this model privileges collective intellectual work that contributes to communal resistance and struggle. In other words, it creatively accents the voluntarism and heroism of the bourgeois model, but it rejects the latter's naiveté about society and history. From the Marxist model, it recovers the stress on structural constraints, class formations, and radical democratic values. Yet the insurgency model does not view these constraints, formations, and values in economistic and deterministic terms. Instead of the *a priori* privileging of the industrial working-class and the metaphysical positing of a relatively harmonious socialist society, there is the wholesale assault on varieties of social hierarchy and the radical democratic (and libertarian) mediation, not elimination, of social heterogeneity. In short, the insurgency model ingeniously incorporates the structural, class, and democratic concerns of the Marxist model, yet it acknowledges the latter's naiveté about culture.

Lastly, from the Foucaultian model, the insurgency model recaptures the preoccupation with worldly skepticism, the historical constitution of "regimes of truth," and the multifarious operations of "power-knowledge." Yet the insurgency model does not confine this skepticism, this truth-constituting and detailed genealogical inquiry to micro-networks of power. Instead of the ubiquity of power (which simplifies and flattens multi-dimensional social conflict) and the paralyzing overreaction to past utopianisms, there is the possibility of effective resistance and meaningful societal transformation. The insurgency model carefully highlights the profound Nietzschean suspicion and the illuminating oppositional descriptions of the Foucaultian model, though it recognizes the latter's naiveté about social conflict, struggle, and insurgency—a naiveté primarily caused by the rejection of any form of utopianism and any positing of a telos.

Black intellectual work and Black collective insurgency must be rooted in the specificity of Afro-American life and history; but they also are inextricably linked to the American, European, and African elements which shape and mold them. Such work and insurgency are explicitly particularist though not exclusivist—hence they are international in outlook and practice. Like their historical forerunners—Black preachers and Black musical artists (with all their strengths and weaknesses)—Black intellectuals must realize that the creation of "new" and alternative practices results from the heroic efforts of collective intellectual work and communal resistance which shape and are shaped by present structural constraints, workings of power, and modes of cultural fusion. The distinctive Afro-American cultural forms such as the Black sermonic and prayer styles, gospels, blues, and jazz should inspire, but not constrain, future Black intellectual production; that is, the process by which they came to be should provide valuable insights, but they should serve as models to neither imitate nor emulate. Needless to say, these forms thrive on incessant critical innovation and concomitant insurgency.

The Future of the Black Intellectual

The predicament of the Black intellectual need not be grim and dismal. Despite the pervasive racism of American society and anti-intellectualism of the Black Community, critical space and insurgent activity can be expanded. This expansion will occur more readily when Black intellectuals take a more candid look at themselves, the historical and social forces that shape them, and the limited though significant resources of the community from whence they come. A critical "self-inventory"—which this essay schematically sets forth—that scrutinizes the social positions, class locations, and cultural socializations of Black intellectuals is imperative. Such scrutiny should be motivated by neither self-pity nor self-satisfaction. Rather this "self-inventory" should embody the sense of critique and resistance applicable to the Black community, American society, and Western civilization as a whole. James Baldwin has noted that the Black intellectual is "a kind of bastard of the West." The future of the Black intellectual lies neither in a deferential disposition toward the Western parent nor a nostalgic search for the African one. Rather it resides in a critical negation, wise preservation, and insurgent transformation of this hybrid lineage which protects the earth and projects a better world.

9

Black Women Intellectuals
by bell hooks

Often I was in some lonesome wilderness, suffering strange things and agonies...cosmic loneliness was my shadow. Nothing and nobody around me really touched me. It is one of the blessings of this world that few people see visions and dream dreams.

Zora Neale Hurston
Dust Tracks on the Road

We have an obligation as Black women to project ourselves into the revolution...

Kay Lindsey
The Black Woman as a Woman

The enormous space that work occupies in Black women's lives today follows a pattern established during the very earliest days of slavery. As slaves, compulsory labor overshadowed every other aspect of women's existence. It would seem, therefore, that the starting point for an exploration of Black women's lives under slavery would be an appraisal of their roles as workers.

Angela Davis
Women, Race, and Class

Living in a society that is fundamentally anti-intellectual, it is difficult for committed intellectuals concerned with radical social change to affirm in an ongoing way that the work we do has meaningful impact. Within progressive political circles, the work of intellectuals is rarely acknowledged as a form of activism, indeed more visible expressions of concrete activism (like picketing in the streets or traveling to a Third World country and other acts of challenge and resistance) are considered more important to revolutionary struggle than the work of the mind. It is this devaluation of intellectual work that often makes it difficult for individuals from marginalized groups to feel that intellectual work is important, that it is a useful vocation. Throughout our history as African Americans in the United States, Black intellectuals have emerged from all classes and conditions of life. However, the decision to consciously pursue an intellectual path has always been an exceptional and difficult choice. For many of us it has seemed more like a "calling" than a vocational choice. We have been moved, pushed, even, in the direction of intellectual work by forces stronger than that of individual will.

Offering an account of the factors that may motivate Black folks to become intellectuals, Cornel West asserts in his essay "The Dilemma of the Black Intellectual," "The choice of becoming a Black intellectual is an act of self-imposed marginality; it assures a peripheral status in and to the Black community. The quest for literacy indeed is a fundamental theme in Afro-American history and a basic impulse in the Black community. But for Blacks, as with most Americans, the uses for literacy are usually perceived to be for more substantive pecuniary benefits than those of the writer, artist, teacher, or professor. The reasons some Black people choose to become serious intellectuals are diverse. But in most cases these reasons can be traced back to a common root: a conversion-like experience with a highly influential teacher or peer that convinced one to dedicate one's life to the activities of reading, writing, and conversing for the purposes of individual pleasure, personal worth, and political enhancement of Black (and often other oppressed) people." Though these may be common reasons Black people choose intellectual work, they may co-exist with motivations that are more difficult to name, especially in public space. In my case, I turned towards intellectual work in a desperate search for an oppositional standpoint that would help me survive a painful childhood. Growing up in a segregated, southern, poor and working-class community where education was valued primarily as a means of class mobility, "intellectual life" was always linked to the career of teaching. It was the outward service as a "teacher" helping to uplift the race, where teachers could gain an individual acceptance within Black community, rather than a privatized, intellectual "inner" life. Growing up in such a world, it was more than evident that there was a socially understood difference between excelling academically and becoming an intellectual. Anyone could teach but not everyone would be an intellectual. And while the role of teacher earned one status and respect, being "too learned," being too intellectual, meant that one risked being seen as weird, strange, and possibly even mad.

Learning early on that good grades were rewarded while independent thinking was regarded with suspicion, I knew that it was important to be "smart" but not "too smart." Being too smart was synonymous with intellectuality and that was cause for concern, especially if one was female. For a smart child in underclass and poor Black communities, to ask too many questions, to talk about ideas that differed from the prevailing community world view, to say things grown Black folks relegated to the realm of the unspeakable was to invite punishment and even abuse. There have yet to be extensive psychoanalytic studies discussing the fate of gifted Black children raised in homes where their brilliance of mind was not valued but made them "freaks" who were persecuted and punished.

During adolescence, I underwent a conversion process that pushed me towards intellectual life. Constantly persecuted and punished in our family, my attempts to understand my lot pushed me in the direction of critical analytical thought. Standing at a distance from my childhood experience, looking at it with a detached disengagement, was for me a survival strategy. To use psychoanalyst Alice Miller's term, I became my own "enlightened witness," able to analyze the forces that were acting upon me, and through that understanding able to sustain a separate sense of my self. Wounded, at times persecuted and abused, I found the life of the mind a refuge, a sanctuary where I could experience a sense of agency and thereby construct my own subject identity. This lived recognition of how the mind engaged in critical thought could be used in the service of survival, how it could be a healing force in my struggle to fight childhood despair enabled me to become an autonomous self in the dysfunctional household and led me to value intellectual work. I valued it not because it brought status or recognition but because it offered resources to enhance survival and my pleasure in living.

Never thinking of intellectual work as being in any way divorced from the politics of everyday life, I consciously chose to become an intellectual because it was that work which allowed me to make sense of my reality and the world around me, to confront and comprehend the concrete. This experience provided the groundwork for my understanding that intellectual life need not lead one to be estranged from community but rather might enable one to participate more fully in the life of family and community. It early confirmed what Black leaders in the 19th century well knew—that intellectual work is a necessary part of liberation struggle, central to the efforts of all oppressed and/or exploited people who would move from object to subject, who would decolonize and liberate their minds.

When Black scholars write about Black intellectual life, they usually focus solely on the lives and works of Black men. Unlike Harold Cruse's massive work *The Crisis of the Negro Intellectual,* which focuses no attention on the work of Black women intellectuals, Cornel West's essay "The Dilemma of the Black Intellectual" was written at a historical moment when there was a feminist focus on gender that should have led any scholar to consider the impact of sex roles and sexism. Yet West does not specifically look at Black female intellectual life. He does not acknowledge the impact of gender or discuss the way sexist notions of male/female roles are factors that inform and shape both our sense of who the Black intellectual is or can be, as well as their relation to a world of ideas beyond individual productions. Despite the historical evidence that Black women have always played a major role as teachers, critical thinkers, and cultural theorists in Black life, particularly in segregated Black communities, there is very little written about Black female intellectuals. When most Black folks think about "great minds" they most often conjure up male images.

Whenever I ask students to name Black intellectuals, without requesting that they be gender-specific, they invariably name Black men: Du Bois, Delaney, Garvey, Malcolm X, and even contemporary folks like Cornel West and Henry Louis Gates are mentioned. If I request that they be gender specific they readily name these Black men and hesitate as they mentally search for the names of Black women. After much pause, they begin to call out the names of famous contemporary Black women writers, usually Alice Walker or Toni Morrison. Now and then Angela Davis's name appears on the list. They do not know the work of 19th century Black women intellectuals. Black women critical thinkers who would be perfect counterparts to Du Bois and Delaney are not known. The names of Anna Julia Cooper, Mary Church Terrell and even the more widely circulated name of Ida B. Wells are not on the tip of everybody's tongue. In her introduction to the Schomburg edition of Anna Julia Cooper's 1892 text *A Voice From The South,* Mary Helen Washington emphasizes both the importance of Black female intellectual work and the reality that it has yet to receive deserved acknowledgement and recognition. Washington asserts: "Without women like Fannie Barrier Williams, Ida B. Wells, Fannie Jackson Coppin, Victoria Earle Matthews, Frances Harper, Mary Church Terrell, and Anna Julia Cooper, we would know very little about the conditions of nineteenth-century Black women's lives, and yet the Black intellectual tradition, until very recently, has virtually ignored them and devalued their scholarship as clearly subordinate to that produced by Black men."

While it is not too surprising that students are unable to name 19th century Black women intellectuals, it is shocking that they do not know the work of contemporary Black women thinkers like Hortense Spillers, Hazel Carby, Patricia Williams, and Beverly Guy-Sheftall, to name a few. Sexist subordination in Black intellectual life continues to obscure and devalue the work of Black female intellectuals. This is why it is so difficult for students to name us. And those students who invoke the names of Walker and Morrison have rarely read their non-fiction work, and often have no clue as to the scope and range of their thought. Black women intellectuals who are not "famous writers" (and not all writers are intellectuals) remain virtually invisible in this society. That invisibility is both a function of institutionalized racism, sexism, and class exploitation, and a reflection of the reality that large numbers of Black women do not choose intellectual work as their vocation.

Working with Black female students within the academy who express extreme reticence about the value and importance of intellectual work has motivated me to critically examine the relationship of Black women to intellectual work, to ask questions: how many Black women would see themselves as being intellectuals? How do we make a living? Are we all in the academy? Where are our essays on intellectual production, etc.? Many of the Black female students I encounter are uncertain about intellectual work. I am awed by the depths of anti-intellectualism they are assaulted by and internalize. Many of them express contempt for intellectual work because they do not see it as having a meaningful connection to "real life" or the realm of concrete experience. Others who are interested in pursuing intellectual work are assailed by doubt because they do not feel there are Black female role models and mentors or they feel the individual Black female intellectuals they encounter do not receive rewards and recognition for their work.

Black female intellectuals working in colleges and universities confront head-on a world that outsiders might imagine would welcome our presence that most often views our intellectuality as "suspect." Folks may be comfortable with the presence of Black female academics and may even desire that presence, but they are less welcoming of Black women who present themselves as committed intellectuals who need institutional support, time, and space to pursue this dimension of their reality. Black woman law professor Patricia Williams in her new collection of essays, *The Alchemy of Race and Rights,* writes eloquently of the way Black female students and professors engage in critical thinking, intellectual work that threatens the status quo and makes it difficult for us to receive necessary support and affirmation. Naming that racism and sexism combined ensures that we will be seen by colleagues with narrow perspectives as intruders. Williams makes it clear that "outsider status is a kind of unresolved wound." Some of us choose then to deny our intellectual ability so as not to confront this reality. Others may choose to be academics but eschew the category "intellectual." In his recent collection of essays *The Significance of Theory*, Terry Eagleton includes an essay "Criticism, Ideology and Fiction," wherein he clarifies the difference between academics (who may or may not be intellectuals) and intellectuals. If one looks at the traditional Western understanding of the intellectual, then it seems to me to be characterized by at least two distinct questions. An intellectual is not simply somebody who trades in ideas. I have many colleagues who trade in ideas whom I'd be extremely reluctant to call intellectuals. An intellectual is somebody who trades in ideas by transgressing discursive frontiers, because he or she sees the need to do that. Secondly, an intellectual is somebody who trades in ideas in their vital bearing on a wider political culture. Eagleton's distinction rests on the assumption of a quality of critical openness that enables transgression. Clearly, he considers it essential that intellectuals be creative thinkers, explorers in the realm of ideas who are able to push to the limits and beyond, following ideas in whatever direction they might take.

It is the sexist/racist Western conception of who and what an intellectual is that rules out the possibility that Black women will come to mind as representatives of intellectual vocation. Indeed, within White supremacist capitalist patriarchy, the entire culture works to deny Black women the opportunity to pursue a life of the mind, makes the intellectual realm a place "off limits." Like our 19th century female ancestors, it is only through active resistance that we claim our right to assert an intellectual presence. Sexism and racism working together perpetuate an iconography of Black female representation that impresses on the collective cultural consciousness the idea that Black women are on this planet primarily for the purpose of serving others. From slavery to the present day, the Black female body has been seen in Western eyes as the quintessential symbol of a "natural" female presence that is organic, closer to nature, animalistic, primitive. Exploring the conflation of woman and nature in *The Death of Nature,* Carolyn Merchant writes:

> The image of nature that became important in the early modern period was that of a disorderly and chaotic realm to be subdued and controlled...wild uncontrollable nature was associated with the female. The images of both nature and woman were two-sided. The virgin nymph offered peace and serenity, the earth mother nurture and fertility, but nature also brought plagues, famines, and tempests. Similarly, woman was both virgin and witch, the Renaissance courtly lover placed her on a pedestal; the inquisitor burned her at the stake. The witch, symbol of the violence of nature, raised storms, caused illness, destroyed crops, obstructed generations, and killed infants. Disorderly woman, like chaotic nature, needed to be controlled.

Among those groups of women murdered as witches in colonial American society, Black females have been historically perceived as embodying a "dangerous" female nature that must be controlled. More so than any group of women in this society, Black women have been seen as "all body, no mind." The use of Black female bodies in slavery as incubators for the breeding of other slaves was the practical exemplification of the notion that "disorderly woman" should be controlled. To justify White male sexual exploitation and rape of Black females during slavery, White culture had to produce an inconography of Black female bodies that insisted on representing them as highly sexed, the perfect embodiment of primitive, unbridled eroticism. Such representations impressed on everyone's consciousness the notion that Black women were all body and no mind. Their cultural currency continues to inform how Black females are perceived. Seen as "sexual sign," Black female bodies are placed in a category that, culturally speaking, is deemed far removed from the life of the mind. Within the sex/race/class hierarchies of the United States, Black women have always resided at the bottom. Lowly status is reserved in this culture for those deemed incapable of social mobility because they are perceived in sexist, racist, and classist terms as deficient, inadequate, inferior.

Overall representations of Black females in contemporary mass media continue to identify us as more sexual, as earthy freakish, out of control. And the popular success of a polemical work like Shahrazad Ali's *The Black Man's Guide to Understanding The Black Woman,* which insists that Black women are the intellectual inferiors of Black men, have smaller brains, etc., indicates the extent to which many Black people internalize sexist/racist thinking about Black female identity. Like those misogynist Renaissance treatises, Ali's book associates Black women with nature, with sexuality, asserting the primary thesis that we must be "controlled."

Running counter to representations of Black females as sexual savages, sluts, and/or prostitutes is the "mammy" stereotype. Again, this image inscribes Black female presence as signified by the body, in this case the construction of woman as mother, as "breast," nurturing and sustaining the life of others. Significantly, the proverbial "mammy" cares for all the needs of others, particularly those most powerful. Her work is characterized by selfless service. Despite the fact that most households in the United States do not have Black maids or nannies working in them, racist and sexist assumptions that Black women are somehow "innately" more capable of caring for others continues to permeate cultural thinking about Black female roles. As a consequence, Black women in all walks of life, from corporate professionals and university professors to service workers, complain that colleagues, co-workers, supervisors, etc. ask them to assume multi-purpose caretaker roles, be their guidance counselors, nannies, therapists, priests; i.e., to be that all nurturing "breast"—to be the mammy. While these Black women are no longer forced by racist exploitative labor practices to "serve" solely in jobs deemed menial, they are still expected to clean up everyone's mess. And it is not simply the White world that brings these expectations to bear on Black women; they are also imposed by Black men and children who also believe that Black women should serve them. Sexist assumptions about women's roles inform the Black communities' expectations of Black women. Many Black folks share the assumptions held by diverse groups in this society that women are "inherently" destined to selflessly serve others. This thinking is often reinforced in Black communities by religious teaching emphasizing the necessity of selfless service as the highest expression of Christian charity. Collectively, many Black women internalize the idea that they should serve, that they should always be available to meet the need of someone else whether they want to or not.

Cultural insistence that Black women be regarded as "service workers" no matter our job or career status as well as Black female passive acceptance of such roles may be the major factor preventing more Black women from choosing to become intellectuals. Intellectual work, even when it is deemed socially relevant, is not seen as "selfless work." Indeed, a prevailing cultural stereotype of an intellectual is someone who is usually self-centeredly preoccupied with their ideas. Even in those cultural arenas where intellectual work is most respected, it is most often seen as work that emerges from self-engagement and self-involvement. Even though Black intellectual men like Du Bois have linked the life of the mind to various forms of political activism, they were self-focused in their pursuit of ideas. Talking with Black women, both academic and non-academic, about our relation to the world of ideas, to seeking knowledge and knowledge production, one of the consistent themes that emerged was the fear of appearing selfish, of not doing work that was seen as directly recognizable as extending beyond the self and "serving" others. Many Black females, myself included, described childhood experiences where the longing to read, contemplate, and talk about a broad range of ideas was discouraged, seen as frivolous activity, or as activity that indulged in too intensely would lead us to be selfish, cold, cut off from feelings and estranged from community. In childhood, if I did not place household chores above the pleasures of reading and thinking, grown-ups threatened to punish me by burning my books, by forbidding me to read. Although this never happened, it impressed on my consciousness the sense that it was somehow not only "wrong" to prefer being alone reading, thinking, writing, but was somehow dangerous to my well-being and a gesture insensitive to the welfare of others. In adulthood, I spent years believing (and therefore making it so) that it was important for me to complete every other task no matter how inconsequential before doing intellectual work.

Of course, I would often arrive at the space intended for such work tired, weary, lacking in energy. Early sexist socialization that teaches Black women, and indeed most women, that mind work must always be secondary to housework, childcare, or a host of other caretaking activities has made it difficult for women to make intellectual work a central priority even when our social circumstances would indeed offer rewards for this activity.

Among Black women thinkers who work as academics, many individuals that I spoke with, felt that their longing to devote time and energy to intellectual work could not be fulfilled because they found themselves perpetually juggling multiple demands. Rightfully complaining that they lack time to pursue intellectual work freely and fully, they also expressed fear that too passionate pursuit of intellectual goals would cut them off from meaningful relational activity. Still, they did not seem eager to interrogate the reasons why they are reluctant, or in some cases downright unable, to claim intellectual work as worthy of primary attention. Focusing particularly on Black females who had completed graduate courses but had stopped at the dissertation writing level, I found they were the most mired in contradictory feelings about the value of academic and/or intellectual work, and that these feelings psychologically blocked their ability to complete this final requirement. It occurred to me that dissertation writing is that moment in one's graduate work where we confront most directly what it means to engage in solitary thinking and writing. For most students, it is that graduate experience which best exemplifies the individualistic character of scholarly thought and work.

One writes alone, usually spending much time in isolation. Often it is difficult to maintain a sense of engagement in community. Black women who have been socialized to devalue or feel guilty about time spent away from others may not be able to claim or create space for isolated writing. This is especially so for Black women who are parents. Single parents must often grapple with concrete material hindrances that do not enable them to focus intensely on thinking and writing even if they so desired. Still, there are individuals without relational or material constraints who are as reluctant as their less advantaged counterparts to claim intellectual work as their primary vocation. Again and again the fear of "isolation" from community or the sense that life was not well lived if not experienced in community was identified as a barrier preventing Black women from wholeheartedly choosing intellectual work. For these barriers to be overcome, individual Black women who are able to remain devoted to an intellectual vocation even as we experience ourselves as connected in community must chart this journey, naming the process.

In "The Dilemma of the Black Intellectual," Cornel West addresses the conflicts that arise when Black intellectuals are faced with a "bourgeois model of intellectual activity" that puts us on the defensive: "There is always the need to assert and defend the humanity of Black people, including their ability and capacity to reason logically, think coherently, and write lucidly. The weight of this inescapable burden for Black students in the White academy has often determined the content and character of Black intellectual activity." These conflicts seem particularly acute for Black women who must also fight against those racist/sexist stereotypes that continually lead others (and even ourselves) to question whether or not we are competent, whether we are capable of intellectual excellence. For Black women scholars and/or intellectuals, writing style may evoke questions of political allegiance. Using a style that may gain one academic acceptance and recognition may further estrange one from a wider Black reading audience. Again, one confronts in a different way questions of isolation and community involvement. Choosing to write in a traditional academic style may lead to isolation. And even if one writes along the lines of accepted academic style there is no guarantee that one's work will be respected.

Often Black thinkers fear our work will not be taken seriously by a larger audience, that it will be seen as lacking in some manner. Such fears inhibit intellectual production. Writing essays that include confessional reflections, I initially felt uncertain about whether they would speak to an audience beyond myself and my friends. When I published my first collection of essays, *Talking Back*, I was surprised by the many letters I received from Black women discussing the essay which focused on the difficulties I faced as a graduate student. Stories of persecution by professors, peers, and professional colleagues poured in. Accounts of Black females being interrogated by those seeking to ferret out whether the individual was capable of completing work, of thinking logically, of writing coherently were a norm. These forms of harassment often undermine Black women's capacity to convey skill and intellectual ability. Then there were the stories—told through letters—of depression and life-threatening despair. Overall, these letters confirm that the choice to pursue an academic and/or intellectual career in the socially legitimate manner continues to be an arduous task for Black females. Even though there are certainly many more Black women academics than ever before, they are often anti-intellectual (a stance which is often a consequence of the pain they have endured as students or as professors who are regarded with suspicion and contempt by peers). In their daily life they may insist that work which speaks directly to concrete experience is more valuable than those forms of intellectual work that are not produced to be marketed to a mass audience. Given the lack of sustained public affirmation and support for Black females choosing intellectual vocations, when confronting such work in isolation, in private spaces, it is not surprising that individual Black women may find themselves overwhelmed by doubts, that such spaces may intensify fears of lack, fears that one's ideas could not possibly be worthy of a hearing. Black women must re-vision notions of intellectual work that enable us to embrace a concern with a life of the mind and the welfare of community.

In "The Dilemma of the Black Intellectual," West is extremely critical of those bourgeois models of intellectual life that conceive of it solely in individualistic or elitist terms, offering the "insurgency" model as an alternative. He asserts: "Instead of the solitary hero, embattled exile, and isolated genius—the intellectual as star, celebrity, commodity—this model privileges collective individual work that contributes to communal resistance and struggle." While the idea of insurgency provides a useful counterpoint to the bourgeois model in theory, West does not address the concrete reality of what circumstances, what material conditions enable and promote intellectual work. Indeed, without privileging the notion of "isolated" genius one must honestly name the reality that much intellectual work takes place in isolation, is informed by time spent in contemplation, revery, and active writing. How can Black women grapple with choosing needed isolation without buying into the bourgeois model? Any discussion of intellectual work that does not emphasize the conditions that make such work possible misrepresents the concrete circumstances that allow for intellectual production. Indeed, Black women struggling to strengthen and deepen our commitment to intellectual work know that we must confront the issue of "isolation," our fear of it, our fear that it estranges us from community inhibits full pursuit of intellectual work. Within patriarchy, men have always had the freedom to isolate themselves from family and community, to do autonomous work and re-enter a relational world when they chose, irrespective of their class status. It is the image of a male figure seeking aloneness to do the work of the mind that is common in mass media, and not that of the female. That patriarchal world which supports and affirms male re-entry into family and community after time apart often punishes females for choosing to do autonomous work. Recent studies (like Arlie Hochschild's *The Second Shift*) which examine the gendered nature of household chores indicate that working women continue to do most housework. So, before that isolated Black woman intellectual can re-enter a relational community, it is likely that she must first assume responsibility for a variety of household chores.

Clearly, Black women academics and intellectuals often are unable to claim necessary alone time to do their work. Discussing the question of isolation with Black women peers and students, I was not surprised to discover that the majority of us had little experience of being alone or working alone. This may be especially true for Black females from poor and working-class backgrounds where limited space and sheer numbers of bodies in a given household made time alone an impossibility. Raised in a large household, it was only when I went to college that I realized I had never been alone a day in my life. Black females raised in sexist households were not placed in situations where we could spend time alone. In fact, it was usually the opposite. We were constantly placed in settings with chaperones or company (in the old days, of course, this was to protect female virtue). Concurrently, it was deemed "unnatural" for a girl who needed to learn how to parent and be a homemaker to spend time alone.

Feminist research on parenting indicates that females are socialized to develop relational skills that enhance our ability to care for others. Such socialization was and is usually made explicit in traditional Black households. Since many Black females have been raised in homes with working mothers, they assumed responsibility for household chores and the care of others early on. Time alone for thinking has not been traditionally valued for Black girls. And even though poor and working-class Black males may not have been raised in settings that overtly valued time alone, males were able to inhabit spaces by themselves, to stand on corners alone and contemplate the universe, sit on rooftops etc. In discussion with other Black females, I found that our time to think usually happened only when domestic chores were done. It was often stolen time. And at times one had to choose between having that space or relational pleasures, hanging out with friends or family. Black women intellectuals know the value of time spent alone. Many Black female thinkers that I interviewed talked about finding it difficult to sit down and write for long stretches of time. Some of this difficulty emerges because individuals may not know how to be comfortable in alone space with alone activity. Certainly not all intellectual work occurs in isolation (some of our best ideas emerge in the context of exchange) but this reality co-exists with the reality that solitary contemplation of ideas is a crucial component of the intellectual process. To feel we have a right to solitary time, Black women must break with conventional sexist/racist notions of woman's role.

Within a White supremacist, capitalist, patriarchal social context like this culture, no Black woman can become an intellectual without decolonizing her mind. Individual Black women may become successful academics without undergoing this process and, indeed, maintaining a colonized mind may enable them to excel in the academy but it does not enhance the intellectual process. The insurgency model that Cornel West advocates, appropriately identifies both the process Black females must engage to become intellectuals and the critical standpoints we must assume to sustain and nurture that choice. To counter the internalized low self-esteem that is constantly actively imposed on Black females in a racist/sexist, anti-intellectual culture, those of us who would become intellectuals must be ever vigilant. We must develop strategies to gain critical assessment of our worth and value that do not compel us to look for critical evaluation and affirmation from the very structures, institutions, and individuals who do not believe in our capacity to learn. Often, we must be able to affirm that the work we do is valuable even if it has not been deemed worthy within socially legitimized structures. Affirming in isolation that work we do can have a meaningful impact in a collective framework, we must often take the initiative in calling attention to our work in ways that reinforce and strengthen a sense of audience.

As a Black woman intellectual writing feminist theory from a standpoint that has as its central scholarly agenda understanding the specific nature of Black gender politics, and as its political task challenging racist and sexist thinking, I began this work in an academic context even though few people in the academy affirmed my efforts. Talking with working-class Black people at various jobs, with folks in the communities I was raised and/or lived in, I found individuals to affirm and encourage my work. This encouragement was crucial to my success. I could not have continued to work in isolation—my spirits would have been depressed. And even though my work is now widely affirmed in academic settings,

I remain most grateful for those non-academic individuals who encouraged me when that support was not there in the socially legitimate place. It is impossible for Black female intellectuals to
blossom if we do not have a core belief in ourselves, in the value
of our work, and a corresponding affirmation from the world
around us that can sustain and nurture. Often we cannot look to
traditional places for recognition of our value; we bear the responsibility for seeking out and even creating different locations.

The politics of patriarchy makes the situation of Black male
intellectuals distinct from that of Black women. Though they confront racism, they do not confront gender biases. And as has already been stated, since they are seen as legitimate members of an
established intellectual tradition, their work is less suspect and
often more rewarded than that of Black women. Importantly, Black
female intellectuals need the support and encouragement of Black
male peers. Often sexism stands in the way of Black males offering
this support. Concurrently, academic competitiveness militates
against the formation of Black intellectual communities that cross
institutions and disciplines. Such communities emerge from the resistance efforts of Black women and men who recognize that we
strengthen our positions by supporting one another.

West insists that "the major priority of Black intellectuals
should be the creation or reactivation of institutional networks that
promote high-quality critical habits primarily for the purpose of
Black insurgency." Taking this proposition a step further, it is crucial that such efforts encompass Black intellectuals who may not
have any formal institutional affiliation. This is especially crucial for
Black women since many exceptional female critical thinkers do
not work in academic settings. Asserting that "the central task of
postmodern Black intellectuals is to stimulate, hasten, and enable
alternative perceptions and practice by dislodging prevailing discourses and powers," West offers a paradigm that allows for an
emphasis on ending sexism and sexist oppression as a necessary
pre-condition for Black intellectual insurgency. For it is only as
Black females and Black males work against the sexist condition-
ing that promotes the assumption that intellectual work is exclusively the domain of males, or that their work is more important,
that we can create communities and environments, that fully promote and sustain our intellectual work. And it is only our vigilant
interrogation of sexist biases and practices that will enable Black
men to encourage and value the work of Black female peers. This
would mean that Black male intellectuals would take our work se-

riously, that they would cease to pay lip-service to the idea of ending sexism while continually ignoring or appropriating ideas. When Black male intellectuals refer to the work of Black female peers and use it constructively in diverse settings (classrooms, lectures etc.), they help bring greater visibility to Black women, strengthening bonds of solidarity. We see this in the work of Black male intellectuals, Manning Marable, Derrick Bell, and Kobena Mercer, to name a few. Concurrently, non-Black allies could best express solidarity by not condoning and supporting Black male appropriation of Black female scholarly labor.

As diverse Black communities grapple with issues of gender, and as the work of feminist scholars is read and/or talked about more widely in such settings, Black female intellectuals will not only have greater recognition and visibility; there will be greater encouragement for young scholars to choose intellectual paths. Despite the many difficulties that surface when Black women choose intellectual work, the possibilities of meaningful reward serve as a counterforce motivating and sustaining us. These rewards may not always be conventional expressions of regard. They may be given by communities who have no contact with academic institutions. Letters from Black men who are in prison and using that time to educate themselves for critical consciousness have been a source of inspiration for my work. When an imprisoned Black male comrade writes me to say, "Your work has touched me in ways that made me strive to be whole," it affirms that intellectual work can connect us with a world outside the academy, can deepen and enrich our sense of community. This is the message I most want to share with young Black females who fear that intellectual work estranges us from the "real" world. In fact, when we do insurgent intellectual work that speaks to a diverse audience, to masses of people with different class, race, or educational backgrounds, we become part of communities of resistance, coalitions that are not conventional. Intellectual work only estranges us from Black communities when we do not relate or share in myriad ways our concerns. That sharing has to go beyond the written word since many Black folks are barely literate or are illiterate. Talking in churches and homes, in both formal and informal ways, we can share the work we do. By acknowledging that reward, understanding, and recognition is, can be, and will be given to us from unconventional places and by valuing these sources of affirmation Black intellectuals call attention to a counter hegemonic system of legitimation and valuation that either in conjunction with the work we do in institutions or as an alternative to it can legitimize and sustain our work.

The affirmation that has come to me from individuals and locations that are on the margins strengthens and inspires me. I call attention to it not to be self-serving but to provide a countertestimony, one that opposes the usual insistence that there can be no meaningful exchange, contact, influence, of intellectuals with everyday folks who may have no educational background. West ends his essay "The Dilemma of the Black Intellectual," with the uplifting comments: "The predicament of the Black intellectual need not be grim and dismal. Despite the pervasive racism of American society and anti-intellectualism of the Black Community, critical space and insurgent activity can be expanded. This expansion will occur more readily when Black intellectuals take a more candid look at themselves, the historical and social forces that shape them, and the limited though significant resources of the community from whence they come." Ongoing critiques of sexism expand that space and make it possible for the contributions of Black women to be valued. Until then, racism and sexism will continue to inform how the work of African American women is regarded.

My awareness of the particular dilemmas Black women intellectuals face was deepened when I began my first full-time teaching job at Yale University. At that time, I was one of two African American women in Yale college. During my stay there the senior Black woman, art historian Sylvia Boone, was tenured. Whenever I called attention to the relative absence of Black women scholars at this institution, naming the impact of sexism and racism, I was told again and again by White male colleagues, "If Black women are not here, it is not because Yale is racist, it is that Black women are simply not good enough." These comments compelled me to critically focus on the ways sexist and racist representations of Black women intellectuals inform the way we are perceived, put in place structures that legitimate the devaluation of our work.

Until my time at Yale, I had not really thought it important or necessary to openly declare myself an "intellectual" and to encourage other Black women to do the same, to make their presence known, to convey our thoughts about the intellectual process. Yearly, I see many brilliant young scholars turn their backs on intellectual work because they feel so diminished in institutions, because they feel their voices are not valued in the larger society. Concern for the future of Black female students, whose intellectual ideas, scholarship and writing are sorely needed has motivated me to do the "critical self-inventory" West advocates and to publically discuss personal experience, giving personal testimony that may encourage and uplift. In the process of critical self-evaluation I realized how I had been socialized not to speak about commitment to intellectual life, but rather to see that as a private, almost "secret" choice. By not speaking about this choice, I was also not conveying to Black female students the joys and pleasures of intellectual work. If I and other Black women, particularly those of us who work in academic settings, only talk about the difficulties, we paint a gloomy picture that may lead students to see intellectual work as diminishing and disenabling. Often in conversations with students, particularly young Black females, I am asked by students to discuss aspects of my personal journeying. This passionate inquiry and interrogation often challenges my sense of privacy (such as it is), yet it is rooted in a profound desire on their part to understand the process by which Black women choose intellectual life, where and how we find personal fulfillment. Their longing for Black women intellectuals to chart the journey often places a demand for openness, for candid, honest revelation that may not be placed on male colleagues, or non-Black women. Yet, Black women intellectuals committed to insurgent practices must recognize the call to speak openly about the intellectual life as we know it, about our work as a form of activism.

Oftentimes intellectual work compels confrontation with harsh realities. It may remind us that domination and oppression continue to shape the lives of everyone, especially Black people and people of color. Such work not only draws us closer to the suffering, it makes us suffer. Moving through this pain to work with ideas that may serve as a catalyst for the transformation of our consciousness, our lives, and that of others is an ecstatic and joyous process. When intellectual work emerges from a concern with radical social and political change, when that work is directed to the needs of the people, it brings us into greater solidarity and community. It is fundamentally life-enhancing.

Selected Bibliography

Baker, Houston A., *Afro-American Poetics: A Revision of Harlem and the Black Aesthetic,* Madison, Wisconsin: University of Wisconsin Press, 1988.

— *Blues, Ideology and Afro-American Literature: A Vernacular Theory,* Chicago: University of Chicago Press, 1984.

— *The Journey Back: Issues in Black Literature and Criticism,* Chicago: University of Chicago Press, 1980.

— *Modernism and the Harlem Renaissance,* Chicago: University of Chicago Press, 1987.

Bambara, Toni Cade, *Gorilla, My Love,* New York: Random House, 1972.

— *The Salt Eaters,* New York: Vintage Books, 1981, c1980.

— *The Seabirds Are Still Alive,* New York: Random House, 1977.

— *Tales and Stories for Black Folks,* Garden City, New York: Zenith Books, 1971.

Baraka, Amina and Amiri Baraka, *Confirmations: An Anthology of African American Women,* New York: Morrow, 1983.

Baraka, Imamu Amiri, *Blues People; Negro Music in White America,* New York: W. Morrow, 1963.

— *Daggers and Javelins: Essays, 1974-1979,* New York: Morrow, 1984.

— *Dutchman and The Slave: Two Plays,* New York: W. Morrow, 1964.

Baudrillard, Jean, *Revenge of the Crystal: Selected Writing on the Modern Object and Its Destiny, 1968-1983,* London and Concord, MA: Pluto Press in association with the Power Institute of Fine Arts, University of Sydney, 1990.

Bell, Derrick A., *Race, Racism, and American Law,* Cambridge, Massachusetts: Harvard Law School, 1970.

— *And We Are Not Saved: The Elusive Quest for Racial Justice,* New York: Basic Books, 1987.

Boggs, James, *Racism and the Class Struggle; Further Pages from a Black Worker's Notebook,* New York: Monthly Review Press, 1970.

— *Manifesto for a Black Revolutionary Party,* Philadelphia: Pacesetters, 1969.

Bogle, Donald, *Blacks in American Films and Television: An Encyclopedia,* New York: Garland Publications, 1988.

— *Brown Sugar: Eighty Years of America's Black Female Superstars,* New York: Harmony Books, 1980.

— *Toms, Coons and Mulattoes, Mammies and Bucks; An Interpretive History of Blacks in American Films,* New York: Viking Press, 1973.

Bontemps, Arna Wendell, editor, *American Negro Poetry,* revised edition, New York: Hill and Wang, 1974.

— *The Harlem Renaissance Remembered: Essays,* New York: Dodd, Mead, 1984, 1972.

Boone, Sylvia Ardyn, *Radiance from the Waters: Ideals of Feminine Beauty in Mende Art,* New Haven: Yale University Press, 1986.

Brooks, Gwendolyn, *Annie Allen,* New York: Harper and Brothers, 1949.

— *Maud Martha, a novel,* New York: Harper, 1953.

— *A Street in Bronzeville,* New York: Harper, 1945.

— *The World of Gwendolyn Brooks,* New York: Harper and Row, 1971.

Cabral, Amilcar, *Return to the Source: Selected Speeches,* New York: Monthly Review Press with Africa Information Service, 1973.

— *Unity and Struggle: Speeches and Writings,* London: Heinemann, 1980.

Carby, Hazel, *Reconstructing Womanhood: The Emergence of the Afro-American Woman Novelist,* New York: Oxford University Press, 1987.

Cesaire, Aime, *The Collected Poetry,* Berkeley: University of California Press, 1983.

Charmichael, Stokely, *Black Power: The Politics of Liberation in America,* with Charles Hamilton, New York: Vintage Books, 1967.

— *Stokely Speaks; Black Power Back to Pan-Africanism,* New York: Random House, 1971.

Clark, John Henrik, editor, *Marcus Garvey and the Vision of Africa,* New York: Random House, 1983.

Clark, Septima Pointsette, *Echo in My Soul,* with LeGette Blythe, New York: Dutton, 1962.

— *Ready from Within: Septima Clark and the Civil Rights Movement,* Navarro, California: Wild Trees Press, 1986.

Collins, Patricia Hill, *Black Feminist Thought: Knowledge, Consciousness, and the Politics of Empowerment,* Boston: Unwin Hyman, 1990.

Cone, James, *Speaking the Truth: Ecumenism, Liberation and Black Theology,* Grand Rapids, Michigan: W.B. Eerdmans Publishing Company, 1986.

— *God of the Oppressed,* New York: Seabury Press, 1975.

— *Martin and Malcolm in America: A Dream or a Nightmare?,* Maryknoll, NY: Orbis Books, 1991.

Crouch, Stanley, *Notes of a Hanging Judge: Essays and Reviews, 1979-1989,* New York: Oxford University Press, 1990.

Cruse, Harold, *The Crisis of the Negro Intellectual,* New York: Morrow, 1967.

— *Rebellion or Revolution?,* New York: Morrow, 1968.

Davis, Angela Yvonne, *Angela Davis—An Autobiography,* New York: Random House, 1974.

— *Women, Culture, and Politics,* New York: Random House, 1989.

— *Women, Race, and Class,* New York: Random House, 1981.

Diop, Cheikh Anta, *Precolonial Black Africa: A Comparative Study of the Political and Social Systems of Europe and Black Africa, from Antiquity to the Formation of Modern States,* Westport, Connecticut: Lawrence Hill, 1987.

— *The African Origin of Civilization: Myth or Reality,* New York: L. Hill, 1974.

— *The Cultural Unity of Black Africa: The Domains of Patrarchy, Matriarchy in Classical Antiquity,* London: Karnak House, 1989.

Douglass, Frederick, *Narrative of the Life of Frederick Douglass, an American Slave,* New York: Penguin Books, 1982.

Drake, St. Clair, *Black Folks Here and There,* Los Angeles: University of California, Los Angeles Press, 1989.

Dubois, W.E.B., *The Gift of Black Folk; The Negroes in the Making of America,* New York: Johnson Reprint, 1968.

— *The Negro in the South: His Economic Progress in Relation to His Moral and Religious Development,* with Booker T. Washington, Philadelphia: G.W. Jacobs, 1907.

Fanon, Frantz, *Black Skin, White Masks,* New York: Monthly Review, 1967.

— *Toward the African Revolution; Political Essays,* New York: Monthly Review Press, 1967.

— *The Wretched of the Earth,* New York: Grove Press, 1965.

Fauset, Jessie Redmon, *The Chinaberry Tree: A Novel of American Life,* New York: Frederick A. Stokes, 1931.

— *Plum Bum,* Boston: Beacon Press, 1990.

— *There is Confusion,* Boston: Northeastern University Press, 1989, c1924.

Frazier, Edward Franklin, *Black Bourgeoisie,* New York: Free Press, 1965.

— *The Negro Church in America,* New York: Schocken Books, 1964, c1963.

— *Race and Culture Contacts in the Modern World,* New York: Knopf, 1957.

Gates, Henry Louis, Jr., editor, *Black Literature and Literary Theory,* New York: Methuen, 1984.

— editor, *The Classic Slave Narratives,* New York: New American Library, 1987.

— *Figures in Black: Words, Signs and the "Racial" Self,* New York: Oxford University Press, 1987.

— editor, *The Schomburg Library of Nineteenth-Century Black Women Writers,* New York: Oxford University Press, 1988.

— *The Signifying Monkey: A Theory of Afro-American Literary Criticism,* New York: Oxford University Press, 1988.

— *Therefore I Am: African American Autobiography,* New York: Pantheon Books, 1990.

Gay, Peter, *The Dilemma of Democratic Socialism; Edward Bernstein's Challenge to Marx,* New York: Columbia University Press, 1952.

Gilroy, Paul, *"There Ain't No Black in the Union Jack": The Cultural Politics of Race and Nation,* London: Hutchinson, 1987.

Haraway, Donna Jeanne, *Primate Visions: Gender, Race and Nature in the World of Modern Science,* New York: Routledge, 1989.

Harper, Francis Ellen and Watkins, Iola Leroy, *Shadows Uplifted,* Boston: Beacon Press, 1987.

Himes, Chester, *A Rage In Harlem,* New York: Vintage Books, 1989, c1957.

— *The Real Cool Killers,* Chatham, N.J.: Chatham Bookseller, 1973, c1959.

— *The Third Generation: A Novel,* New York: Thunder's Mouth Press, 1989.

hooks, bell, *Ain't I a Woman,* Boston, MA: South End Press, 1981.

— *Feminist Theory: From Margin to Center,* Boston, MA: South End Press, 1984.

— *Talking Back: Thinking Feminist, Thinking Black,* Boston, MA: South End Press, 1989.

— *Yearning: Race, Gender, and Cultural Politics,* Boston, MA: South End Press, 1990.

Hurston, Zora Neale, *Dust Tracks on a Road; An Autobiography,* Philadelphia: Lippincott, 1971, c1942.

— *I Love Myself When I Am Laughing...and Then Again When I Am Looking Mean and Impressive: A Zora Neale Hurston Reader,* Old Westbury, New York: The Feminist Press, 1979.

— *Spunk: The Selected Stories of Zora Neale Hurston,* Berkeley, CA: Turtle Island Foundation, 1985.

— *Tell My Horse: Voodoo and Life in Haiti and Jamaica,* New York: Perennial Library, 1990.

— *Their Eyes Were Watching God; A Novel,* Westport Connecticut: Greenwood Press, 1969, c1937.

Jackson, George, *Soledad Brother: The Prison Letters of George Jackson,* New York: Coward-McCann, 1970.

Jacobs, Harriet, *Incidents in the Life of a Slave Girl,* New York: Harcourt, Brace, Jovanovich, 1973.

James, C.L.R., *Beyond a Boundary,* New York: Pantheon Books, 1963.

— *The Black Jacobins; Toussaint L'Ouverture and the San Domingo Revolution,* New York: Vintage Books, 1963.

— *Notes on Dialectics: Hegel, Marx, Lenin,* London: Alison and Busby, 1980.

Jeffers, Susan J., *Feel the Fear and Do It Anyway,* San Diego: Harcourt Brace Jovanovich, 1987.

Jordan, June, *Civil Wars,* Boston: Beacon Press, 1981.

— *Living Room: New Poems,* New York: Thunder's Mouth Press, 1985.

— *Moving Towards Home: Political Essays,* London: Virago, 1989.

— *On Call: Political Essays,* Boston: South End Press, 1985.

Kincaid, Jamaica, *Annie John,* New York: Farrar, Straus, Giroux, 1985.

— *Lucy,* New York: Farrar, Straus, Giroux, 1990.

— *A Small Place,* New York: Farrar, Straus, Giroux, 1988.

King, Martin Luther, Jr., *The Measure of a Man,* Philadelphia: Christian Education Press, 1959.

— *The Trumpet of Conscience,* New York: Harper and Row, 1968.

— *Where Do We Go from Here: Chaos or Community?,* New York: Harper and Row, 1967.

— *Why We Can't Wait,* New York: Harper and Row, 1964.

King, Martin Luther, Sr., *Daddy King: An Autobiography,* New York: Morrow, 1980.

Larsen, Nella, *Quicksand and Passing,* New Brunswick, N.J.: Rutgers University Press, 1986.

Lee, Don L., *Black Pride, Poems,* Detroit: Broadside Press, 1968.

— *Directionscore: Selected and New Poems,* Detroit, Broadside Press, 1971.

— *Don't Cry; Scream,* Detroit: Broadside Press, 1969.

— *Dynamite Voices,* Detroit: Broadside Press, 1971.

— *From Plan to Planet: Life Studies,* Detroit: Broadside Press, 1973.

— *Think Black,* Detroit: Broadside Press, 1967.

— *We Walk the Way of The New World,* Detroit: Broadside Press, 1970.

Lorde, Audre, *Between Ourselves,* Point Reyes, California: Eidolon Editions, 1976.

— *The Black Unicorn: Poems,* New York: Norton, 1978.

— *A Burst of Light: Essays,* Ithaca, New York: Firebrand Books, 1988.

— *Cables to Rage,* London: P. Breman, 1970.

— *The Cancer Journals,* Argyle, New York: Spinsters Ink, 1980.

— *Chosen Poems, Old and New,* New York: Norton, 1982.

— *The First Cities,* New York City: Poets Press, 1968.

— *From a Land Where Other People Live,* Detroit: Broadside Press, 1973.

— *Our Dead Behind Us: Poems,* New York: Norton, 1986.

— *Sister Outsider: Essays and Speeches,* Trumansberg, NY: Crossing Press, 1984.

— *Zami, A New Spelling of My Name,* Watertown, Massachusetts: Persephone Press, 1982.

Lukacs, Gyorgy, *History and Class Consciousness; Studies in Marxist Dialectics,* Cambridge, Massachusetts: MIT Press, 1971.

Madhubuti, Haki R., *Black Men: Obsolete, Single, Dangerous?: Afrikan American Families in Transition: Essays in Discovery, Solution, and Hope,* Chicago: Third World Press, 1990.

Marable, Manning, *Race, Reform, and Rebellion: The Second Reconstruction in Black America, 1945-1982,* Jackson: University Press of Mississippi, 1984.

—*How Capitalism Underdeveloped Black America,* Boston: South End Press, 1983.

— *Toward Independent Black Politics,* Dayton, Ohio: Black Research Associates, 1981.

Marshall, Paule, *Brown Girl, Brownstones,* Chatham, N.J.: Chatham Bookseller, 1972, c1959.

— *The Chosen Place, The Timeless People,* New York: Harcourt, Brace and World, 1969.

— *Praisesong for the Widow,* New York: Putnam's, 1983.

Marx, Karl, Frederick Engels, *Collected Works,* New York: International Publishers, 1975.

— *The Poverty of Philosophy,* New York: International Publishers, 1936.

Memmi, Albert, *The Colonizer and the Colonized,* New York: Orion Press, 1965.

Morrison, Toni, *Beloved: A Novel,* New York: Knopf: Distributed by Random House, 1987.

— *The Bluest Eye,* New York: Holt, Rinehart, and Winston, 1970.

— *Song of Solomon,* New York: Knopf: Distributed by Random House, 1977.

— *Sula,* New York: Knopf: Distributed by Random House, 1973.

— *Tar Baby,* New York: Knopf: Distributed by Random House, 1981.

Mudimbe, V.Y., *Before the Birth of the Moon,* New York: Simon and Schuster, 1989.

Naylor, Gloria, *Linden Hills,* New York: Ticknor and Fields, 1985.

— *Mama Day,* New York: Ticknor and Fields, 1988.

— *The Women of Brewster Place,* New York: Viking Press, 1982.

Nichols, Charles H., editor, *Arna Bontemps-Langston Hughes Letters, 1925-1967,* New York: Dodd, Mead, 1980.

Petry, Ann Lane, *Miss Muriel and Other Stories,* Boston, 1971.

— *The Narrows,* Chatham, N.J.:Chatham Bookseller, 1973.

— *The Street,* New York: Pyramid Books, 1975, c1946.

Raboteau, Albert J., *Slave Religion: "The Invisible Institution" in the Antebellum South,* New York: Oxford University Press, 1978.

Rodney, Walter, *How Europe Underdeveloped Africa,* revised edition, Washington, D.C.: Howard University Press, 1981.

Rogers, J.A., *Sex and Race: Why White and Black Mix in Spite of Opposition,* New York: Helga A. Rogers, 1942-72.

Said, Edward W., *After the Last Sky: Palestinian Lives,* London; Boston: Faber and Faber, 1986.

— *Beginnings: Intention and Method,* New York: Basic Books, 1975.

— *Covering Islam: How the Media and Experts Determine How We See the Rest of the World,* New York: Pantheon Books, 1981.

Shange, Ntozake, *Betsey Brown: A Novel,* New York: St. Martin's Press, 1985.

— *For Colored Girls Who Have Considered Suicide When the Rainbow is Enuf,* San Lorenzo, CA: Shameless Hussy Press, 1975.

— *Sassafras, Cypress, and Indigo: A Novel,* New York: St. Martin's Press, 1982.

Smith, Barbara, editor, *Homegirls: A Black Feminist Anthology,* New York: Kitchen Table—Women of Color Press, 1983.

Smith, Valerie, *Self-Discovery and Authority in Afro-American Narrative,* Cambridge, Massachusetts: Harvard University Press, 1987.

Spelman, Elizabeth, *Inessential Woman: Problems of Exclusion in Feminist Thought,* Boston: Beacon Press, 1988.

Spivak, Gayatari Chakravorty, *In Other Worlds: Essays in Cultural Politics,* New York: Methuen, 1987.

— *The Post Colonial Critic: Interviews, Strategies, Dialogues,* New York: Routledge, 1990.

Taussig, Michael T., *Shamanism, Colonialism, and the Wild Man: A Study in Terror and Healing,* Chicago: University of Chicago Press, 1986, c1987.

Thompson, Robert Farris, *Flash of the Spirit: African and Afro-American Art and Philosophy,* New York: Random House, 1983.

Walker, Alice, *The Color Purple,* New York: Washington Square Press, 1982.

— *In Search of Our Mother's Gardens: Womanist Prose,* San Diego: Harcourt Brace Jovanovich, 1983.

— *Living by the Word: Selected Writings,* 1973-1987, San Diego: Harcourt Brace Jovanovich, 1988.

— *The Temple of My Familiar,* San Diego: Harcourt Brace Jovanovich, 1989.

Wallace, Michele, *Black Macho and the Myth of the Superwoman,* New York: Dial Press, 1979.

— *Invisibility Blues: From Pop to Theory, New York: Verso, 1990.*

Washington, James Melvin, *Frustrated Fellowship: The Black Baptist Quest for Social Power,* Georgia: Mercer University Press, 1986.

West, Cornel, *The American Evasion of Philosophy: A Genealogy of Pragmatism,* Macon, Madison, Wisconsin: University of Wisconsin Press, 1989.

— *The Ethical Dimensions of Marxist Thought,* New York: Monthly Review Press, 1991.

— *Prophesy Deliverance! An Afro-American Revolutionary Christianity,* Philadelphia: Westminster Press, 1982.

— *Prophetic Fragments,* Grand Rapids, Michigan: Eerdmans, 1988.

White, Evelyn C., editor, *The Black Women's Health Book: Speaking for Ourselves,* Seattle, WA: Seal Press, 1990.

Williams, Patricia J., *The Alchemy of Race and Rights,* Cambridge, Massachusetts: Harvard University Press, 1991.

Willis, Susan, *Specifying: Black Women Writing the American Experience,* Madison, Wisconsin: University of Wisconsin Press, 1987.

Wilson, Harriet, *Our Nig, or Sketches in the Life of a Free Black, in a Two-story White House, Showing that Slavery's Shadows Fall Even There,* New York: Random House, 1983.

Wright, Richard, *American Hunger,* New York: Harper and Row, 1977.

— *Black Boy: A Record of Childhood and Youth,* New York: Harper and Row, 1945.

— *Black Power; A Record of Reactions in a Land of Pathos,* New York: Harper, 1954.

— *The Long Dream: A Novel,* Garden City: Doubleday and Company, 1958.

— *Native Son,* New York: Harper and Brothers, 1940.

X, Malcolm, *The Autobiography of Malcolm X,* New York: Grove Press, 1965.

— *Malcolm X on African American History,* New York: Pathfinder Press, 1970.

— *Malcom X: The Last Speeches,* New York: Pathfinder Press, 1989.

— *The Speeches of Malcolm X at Harvard,* New York: Morrow, 1968.

About South End Press

South End Press is a nonprofit, collectively run book publisher with over 150 titles in print. Since our founding in 1977, we have tried to meet the needs of readers who are exploring, or are already committed to, the politics of radical social change.

Our goal is to publish books that encourage critical thinking and constructive action on the key political, cultural, social, economic, and ecological issues shaping life in the United States and in the world. In this way, we hope to give expression to a wide diversity of democratic social movements and to provide an alternative to the products of corporate publishing.

If you would like a free catalog of South End Press books or information about our membership program—which offers two free books and a 40% discount on all titles—please write us at South End Press, 116 Saint Botolph Street, Boston, MA 02115.

Other titles of interest from South End Press:

Yearning: Race, Gender, and Cultural Politics
bell hooks

Feminist Theory, from margin to center
bell hooks

Talking Back: Thinking Feminist, Thinking Black
bell hooks

Ain't I a Woman: black women and feminism
bell hooks

Black Looks
bell hooks

Pipe Dream Blues: Racism and the War on Drugs
Clarence Lusane

How Capitalism Underdeveloped Black America
Manning Marable